AF255759

THE
BOY
Who Hated
NUMBERS

J.R. ARRANGUEZ JR.

DIAMOND MEDIA PRESS CO.
1-304-273-6157
https://www.diamondmediapressco.com/

ISBN Paperback: **978-195436821-7**

CONTENTS

Acknowledgment

I'd like to thank again Ms. Teresa Brantley of the Wake County Public School System for sharing me her ideas in writing a children's book.

In those years that I worked in the NC Department of Revenue in Raleigh, if I encountered a mean few, I also met people who treated me cordially notwithstanding my being a minority. Somehow, they inspired me to write 'Reminiscence', a book about the aspirations and frustrations, the triumphs and failures, the glory and passion, and the joy and sorrow that immigrants had gone through in this country they dreamed of as paradise.

I miss those nice and friendly fellow workers of NC-DOR in Raleigh. I can only name a few to thank for. Their warmth and sincerity is something I'd like to treasure through the years.

Thanks to Wilma Hopkins and Karen Gamble of DP-PD's Exception unit; Erlinda Yatta, Khushman Surti, and Vivian Rainey of the Registration unit; Eloisa Chaika, Helen Faulcon, Ellen Johnson, Shannon Jones, and Cynthia Oates of the Central Collections Unit. Their kindness is always remembered.

If I were to mention the most wonderful executives I worked with in NCDOR Raleigh, Kim Sabol, director of Taxpayers Division, definitely tops them all. My list wouldn't be complete without the names of Debbie Wall and Diana Salmon (both retired), former group managers of the Exception/registration Unit of DPPD. Ditto with the former NCDOR secretary Reginald Hinton and deputy secretary Keith McCombs. Forever, I keep their friendship with great pride and honor.

Like a novel, if there are protagonists there are also antagonists. If I'm grateful to some people for their kindness, I'm also grateful to the unkind few who loved to bully me around while I was at work. They caused me to quit my job, eventually. Rude as they were, somehow, they gave me ideas on how to define well the villains in my upcoming books. Thus, I'd like to extend my thanks to these people for their harassments were factors that defied me to seek success in another field of endeavor.

DEDICATIONS

For my spouse, Edna; my daughter, Gypsy Rose; my elder son, Jiffy Jon; and my youngest child, Rez Robby, who gave me ideas in creating the character of Rebmun, the boy who hated numbers.

My family had been always there for me, keeping me up with encouragements whenever I was 'down and troubled'. Without my children's persuasions, I couldn't have written this book.

Special dedication goes to my first grandchild. Ryleigh Akemi Arranguez Shimizu was born on June 12, 2020.

Preface

Somewhere in the remote areas of Western North *Carolina, in a tiny village called Moon Cap, dwelt a man who believed that a person's fate is shaped up with numbers. Named after one of the greatest mathematicians of all time, Newton Reed lived with his wife, Reba and a son he named 'number' spelled backward.*

As Newton loved numbers, he thought that so was his son. On the contrary, the boy was slow where his parents expected him to excel. This proved very disappointing to them so they hired a tutor to help their son stand out in arithmetic, and a nanny to take care of him in his daily needs.

Yet to Rebmun those weren't good substitutes to the companionship he needed. The boy felt neglected for both parents were very much involved in their respective careers, their sports and other social activities.

Knowing how his parents wanted him to be outstanding in mathematics, Rebmun started to hate numbers in defiance. He refused to learn anything about numbers.

Eventually, his disobedience worked to his disadvantage; the boy developed a real abhorrence for numbers.

During weekdays after school, Rebmun confined himself in his room. He wasn't free to watch TV or talk with friends on the phone as much as he wanted. Only with Miles, the English-Setter dog that his parents gifted him on his seventh birthday, could he freely tell his dreams and ambitions and relate his adventures in school. Miles was faithfully keeping him company, but the dog could only bark in response.

In some other times, Rebmun would watch from the window in his room the forest of Deervana which looked gray at a distance. It was known to be enchanted. Pets who ran away from their cruel masters and sought shelter in this forest had never returned.

It had been Rebmun's plan to uncover the mystery hidden there even if his parents were constantly reminding him never to come near to it. The more they warned him, the more curious Rebmun had become to find what's inside the forest of Deervana.

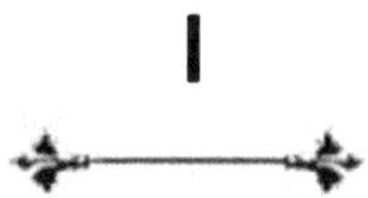

One Saturday morning, believing that his parents had gone out of the village for a day, Rebmun decided to explore the forest of Deervana. It had been his longtime plan and now, he thought it's a perfect day to carry it out. With a backpack of things he needed for a day away from home, Rebmun pulled out his bike and followed Miles who was following a trail that led to the forest of Deervana.

It was a clear day when the boy sat out but unfortunately to Rebmun, the weather changed. In less than a mile away from home, the boy noticed a thick rain clouds had gathered over the forest. Anticipating a heavy downpour that could ruin definitely his entire journey, Rebmun decided to terminate his plan. He called Miles and told the dog to go back home. The dog stopped and turned around as if to ask his master why the sudden change of plan.

"There's a heavy rain coming," Rebmun told his pet half-shouting. "We just have to backtrack and postpone this journey on some other time. Summer vacation is coming anyway and we have lots of time for this journey."

Rebmun turned around his bike and raced with Miles back home. In the driveway, the boy was surprised to see his parents' car.

"I thought you and Dad are out for a day," Rebmun said upon seeing his mother.

"That's what we planned, but on the way we got a call from your dad's friend informing us that our trip was cancelled and postponed to another Saturday," Reba explained. "The call was late but as the saying goes . . ."

". . . It's better late than never."

"You got it! By the way, you weren't around when we came home. Where have you been?"

"I was playing with Miles at the back, a little bit away from the house."

"That's fine, as long as it's far away from the forest. As I told you before, don't go near to that forest, not even within a mile. It must be inhabited with creepy creatures. Just yesterday, another boy from the next town got missing, believed to have gone to the forest in search of his lost pet. Both the boy and his pet dog didn't return home anymore."

"I know about it, Mom; in fact I knew the boy personally. Jim Connerton had been a friend when we had our scout Jamboree in Raleigh last year."

"So, you've heard about what happened to Jim. Now, you have the reason to be extra careful even if you're just outside of the house. The forest is about four miles away and it's possible that those creepy creatures living there could go out of the forest to look for victims."

"I'm careful about it, Mom," said Rebmun. "The farthest that Miles and I had gone playing was half-a-mile away from home, right Miles?"

Reba turned to Miles and said: "You heard my words, Miles and I hope you, too, must be careful of yourself. Also, I trust that you will watch over your best friend. Remember he's the only friend you have."

The dog barked again and jumped at Rebmun, licking the boy's face.

"Okay, that's fine. Now, Rebmun, do you remember what day is today?"

"It's a Saturday," Rebmun said laughing. "I may not be good in counting numbers but not bad in counting days. Kids in school know it well that Saturday follows Friday."

"Yes, it's a Saturday, but do you remember the importance of this day?"

"Of course, . . . it's my birthday."

"On our way back home, we bought something you'd drool over."

"Don't you think I'm already old to play with toys?"

"It's not a toy; it's much better."

"What is it? Tell me what it is."

"Aside from your favorite birthday cake, your dad brought you a bird; a real one . . ."

"A bird?" Rebmun looked disappointed.

"Yes! A parrot . . . "

It was Newton Reed who replied. He was coming out from the garage with a golden cage hanging from his right hand. Inside the cage was a parrot with a short hooked bill and a plumage of vivid green.

"You know I don't appreciate parrots. They're the noisiest ones and the most boring."

"Well, this isn't an ordinary parrot. You'll find this very different."

Rebmun stared at the bird and after a few seconds, with a glint of amusement flashing in his eyes, asked: "Is it a boy or a girl?"

"The store clerk said it's a boy," answered the father. "This is the weirdest you'd ever know. The bird can talk."

"He can? Where did he come from?"

"I got it from Patrick's pets, but that comes from the Philippines, according to Mr. Patrick," said Newton Reed. "It cost a lot but that's fine because you rarely can find a parrot that can talk like human. It's the most wonderful present yet we ever had gifted."

"Definitely, it is! I learned in school that the Philippines is a far-away land across a large ocean. That's impossible if this parrot comes from there? Does he talk in our language?"

"Yes, he does," Newton replied.

Rebmun walked nearer to his father and stared closely at the bird in the cage as if studying something about it. The bird was standing still and at the same time keeping an eye at the boy. It had been intently listening to the family's conversation.

"Good morning," the boy greeted the bird.

"Good morning," the bird greeted back.

"Indeed! This bird can really talk!" Rebmun exclaimed. "It's amazing! "

"Ask him his name," said Rebmun's Mom.

"Hey, what's your name, buddy?"

"Poutric . . ." replied the bird.

Rebmun roared with laughter. "Poutric! Are you kidding me? That's the funniest name I ever heard."

"I got him from Patrick's Pets so maybe, he thinks his name is Patrick. The bird doesn't have a name yet."

"Pets always have names. I'd like to give him a name."

"Any name you think that fits him," said Newton Reed.

The thought that the bird could talk well like a human made the boy over excited. He was having this thing to talk to whenever he was alone and got bored in his room. The boy didn't know that his parents had other plans for the bird to do. The bird could count numbers like a real pro.

Home to the multicolored lorikeet was a gold colored cage that would be hanging by the window in Rebmun's room. Every morning at six on school days, the boy could hear the sharp shrill voice of the bird, waking him up by shouting out "it's six o'clock" twice like a cuckoo clock. If the boy didn't get out of bed by six, the bird started counting up numbers and would only stop if Miles got annoyed and barked at him to shut up.

These morning activities of the English-Setter dog and the parrot were quite amusing to Rebmun but after a few days that the bird did the same routine, it occurred to the boy that the bird was up for something.

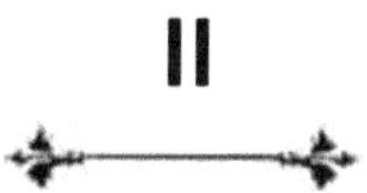

The parrot's morning ritual was amusing to Reb-mun the first few days. The boy grew fond of the bird that he'd be hurrying home when classes were over to tell the bird of his adventures in school.

On weekends, Rebmun was enjoying the company of his pets that he longed no more for his parents' attention.

One Friday afternoon after school, Rebmun engaged the bird to a long conversation.

"Hey, buddy, Miles got his name from me and you know what, I'm thinking of also giving you a name."

"A new name for me!" the lorikeet exclaimed and danced around inside his cage in appreciation of the boy's gesture in giving him importance.

"You heard it right. I'll give you a name."

"That's nice of you, master. What is it?"

"You're a lorikeet, so I'll call you Loro."

"Loro for a lorikeet . . . That sounds good," the bird said. "I also think of giving you a name, master."

"I don't need it; I already have one . . ."

"I want to give you a name that's easy for me to remember."

"Shoot . . . and what is it, Loro?"

"I'm rousing you up at six in the morning so I'd like to call you Master Six O'clock."

"It's a queer name but I can live with it."

"Well and good!"

"By the way, my friend, may I know where did you come from?"

"Why did you ask, Six O'clock?"

"Dad said you come from the Philippines. I don't think you were from there. Come on, buddy, tell me . . ."

"Does it matter?"

"But the Philippines is a very far-away land across a wide ocean."

"You really want to know?"

"If you won't mind; I'm curious about it."

"Well if you insist to know, Mister Six O'clock, I will tell you," the bird said.

Rebmun waited for Loro to say something, but the bird fell silent. It seemed he didn't want to reveal his place of origin.

"Say it. No one's listening, but me."

"Okay, I come not from the Philippines but from another faraway land."

"Go on," Rebmun said when he noticed the bird's hesitation.

"But this must be kept a secret."

"I promise," Rebmun immediately replied twisting at the same time his index and middle fingers in his eagerness to hear what the bird was about to reveal.

"Well, somebody must have misheard the name of the place I came from."

"So, where did you really come from?"

"I come not from the Philippines but from the *Field of Pines*."

"The field of pines . . . that's strange."

"No human had reached that place yet."

"And you came from there . . ."

". . . Born and raised, born and raised."

"Where in the world is it? Is it far or near to the forest of Deervana?"

"Don't know where's that, but the Field of Pines is just near you that you can almost touch it yet so far that you can't see it."

"That sounds like a dream."

"What's a dream?" asked the lorikeet.

"You don't know what a dream is? Haven't tried dreaming?"

"I won't be asking if I know . . .

"It's this event that plays in your mind while you're sleeping."

"That's queer."

"Some dreams are vivid they seem to be real but confusing they don't even make sense," Rebmun explained.

"So, they're not real?" Loro's curiosity was rising.

"They're gone like smoke when the dreamer wakes up. Some dreams come true, some people say."

"That's exciting, but how? Why? When?"

"That's confusing to you as of now. We better change the topic, Loro."

"Okay, what is it? What is it?"

"My dad got you from a pet store, remember?"

"But I don't know how I ended up there."

"What's the last thing you remember?"

"I ran away one day when Varcoba attacked the *Field of Pines*."

"Who's Varcoba?"

"She's a kind of devil who often attacks the Field of Pines in her search for something. So, when she attacked our kingdom again . . ."

"Always the *Field of Pines* of all places? What is she searching for?"

"According to Yorka, Varcoba is in search of the amygdaloid amulet which Yorka had been keeping. Varcoba wants to own the amulet because of the power it had."

"And who's Yorka?" Rebmun asked even if it seemed to him that Loro was making up characters and building a tall tale.

"He was the most senior denizen in the *Field of Pines;* the keeper of the amygdaloid amulet that's giving our kingdom protection against evil."

"Interesting . . . continue talking, Loro."

"Our race was believed to get extinct by the end of the millennium, but that didn't happen because we have Yorka's talisman."

"Okay, I'm listening . . ."

"It's the only thing that links the zobuses to the human world."

". . . and what are zobuses?"

"We, the inhabitants of the *Field of Pines.*"

"Go on . . . I'm listening . . ."

"Yorka was the trusted keeper of the amulet. Kingdoms from the dark world invaded the *Field of Pines* in their desire to steal the talisman. If we lose the amulet, the Kingdom of Dome and its inhabitants would be gone like a dream."

"But how did the other kingdoms know about this amulet?"

"That's what I want to find out. Yorka didn't tell me how these things started."

"Okay, you may continue."

"When Yorka foresaw another invasion he hid the amulet in his mouth. That   transformed him into a giant blue eagle. His wings were covered not by plumes but blue daggers."

"Loro, are you sure this isn't a myth?"

"If you don't believe me, I can't tell you no more," said the bird; he was getting upset.

"Sorry, Loro. Please continue but make your story a little bit believable."

"Don't ever interrupt me again."

Rebmun crossed his fingers, "Promise".

"As I said, Yorka transformed himself into a bird, a huge blue eagle. As such, he would be flying around the Dome."

"What did he do that for?"

"To warn the zobuses of a coming danger."

"Wow! Like the guardian of the people; like Superman."

"Yorka was said to be invincible but there was a spot in his spine that would render him vulnerable . . ."

"Okay, I'm listening . . ."

"One day, I saw him lying in the woods face down with a large wound in his spine; he was stabbed and was bleeding to death."

"By who? Who did that?"

"Yorka didn't see who did it," the bird replied. "But we had suspicions that the culprit was a zobus."

"He must be somebody that had known Yorka so well because he knew the danger spot in Yorka's backbone," the boy suggested.

"Yes, must be a zobus. Before Yorka lost his life, he trusted the amulet to me and told me how to handle it."

"That means Yorka left you the responsibility of safeguarding your tribe."

"Yorka didn't at all leave the kingdom right that moment."

"I thought you said he died."

"He died but his spirit came one night to warn me that the kingdom was facing a coming danger."

"What was it? What was it, Loro?" Rebmun asked looking confused.

"When a full moon rises for the last time of the century Varcoba was coming again with her guzzlers to wreak havoc to our race."

"Guzzlers? What are guzzlers?"

"The giant vultures that have the fierce of a hungry lion. They're identified with their forked horns and monstrous red eyes."

"Like vampires . . ." Rebmun deduced.

"Yes, they feed themselves with blood - animal blood, according to Yorka."

"And there were only thirteen of them?"

"Only thirteen but have the force of thirteen hundred. Yorka said the guzzlers are ageless and immortal."

Rebmun's doubt about Loro grew stronger. He thought he needed to know more of the bird's credibility. The boy thought there was no use of talking to the bird; it would result to nothing so he decided to end up his conversation with the bird.

"I'm getting sleepy, Loro. I think it's better for the two of us to get a good sleep, a real good sleep to clear our minds."

"Did I get you bored, master?"

"No, not at all," Rebmun replied while forcing himself to yawn.

"Are you doubting of what I told you? Don't you believe what I told you?"

"You're telling me your dreams and you said you never ever have a dream in your life."

"I never had. I don't remember dreaming of anything. The zobuses don't have that talent."

"It's not a talent, Loro," the boy replied. He stood still and for a moment stared at the bird. "Now tell me, are you really a bird or a human?"

"I'm a zobus trapped in a bird's body."

Loro's reply made the boy more confused, didn't take his eyes off of Loro, but wasn't saying a word.

The bird avoided Rebmun's eyes. "I know it. Now you think something's wrong with me. I know it."

"I'm not thinking of that," the boy responded.

"Then, what do you think about me?" Loro asked with his eyes now nailed at the boy.

"I think you need a long good sleep."

Rebmun walked to his bed to avoid further conversation with the bird.

"Wait, Master Six O'clock. There's something more I want to tell you."

"I don't want to listen about it, Loro for it seems you're disoriented. You need to give yourself a good, good rest. Good night."

Early the following Saturday morning, before Loro could wake him up, Rebmun had already risen up from bed. He was looking forward to spending the day playing with Miles.

"Good morning," Rebmun greeted his pets. "Sorry, Loro for what I said last night."

"Forget about it," the bird replied. "By the way, Master, may I ask, why do you always say 'Good morning'?"

"Out of habit; my parents always say that every morning on seeing me."

"Who started this thing?"

"I don't know who did. It was there one day when I woke up to the world; it's how people greet each other in the morning."

"That was what your dad said to me when he came to the store."

"Wherever you go, people you meet will greet you with good morning. You'd always hear people say this thing in the morning and you can't help it but say the same thing in return out of respect," said the boy. "Well, how's your morning, buddy?"

"As wonderful as the morning outside."

"It's a beautiful day to play with Miles."

"It's always Miles; how about me?"

"You can't play ball. Just watch us by the window from your cage."

"It's unfair. You can't just lock me inside the cage. I also need to energize my body."

"Maybe one of these days I'll set you free for a day to exercise your wings but not now."

"Okay, you're the master but remember your promise to set me free for a day."

"I promise, Loro."

"One question: Did I get you bored last night?" the bird asked.

"Not bored, but I just found your story strange and confusing."

". . . I know. It's as strange as a dream and you'd doubt about it unless you had seen yourself the place I came from . . ."

". . . which seems not existing."

"I can't force you to believe it."

"You said you already had Yorka's amulet. Then what did you do when your world was assaulted?"

"Varcoba was after of the amulet so I hid it in my mouth. Unexpectedly, after doing that I became a lorikeet as Yorka turned into an eagle when he hid the amulet inside his mouth."

"Why a lorikeet and not a blue eagle?"

"How should I know?"

"What happened then?" asked Rebmun.

"I tried to escape away from the *Field of Pines.* I was already flying far up in the air when something hard hit me on the head. That's all I remembered. I passed out and when I woke up I was in a cage in a place where people come and go."

"Yeah . . . that was the pet store."

"One morning, a man came looking for a parrot that can talk."

"That was my dad."

"He came to me and said 'good morning'. Out of reflex I repeated his words. Then I was taken out of the cage and . . ."

"My father brought you here. Aren't you glad you're here and got a friend to talk to?"

"I am but look, I'm still in a cage. In the world I came from, I was free, free to roam around, free to gather my own food."

"You said that the *Field of Pines* is just so near yet so far away that I can't see it, what do you mean by that?"

"You have to close your eyes to see it and think of it to reach it."

"I don't understand what you're saying."

"You don't understand as of now. You've got to see first the Kingdom of Dome . . ."

"I don't know how can that be possible."

"Yes, you can. Everybody is welcome there – humans or non-humans."

"I don't even know where in the world that field is."

"As I told you just think of it to reach it."

"How can I think of it when I don't know what

does it look like."

"Imagine it to see it in however you wish."

"Okay, if I go there for real, am I safe?"

"You know that danger is lurking everywhere. Tell me first, am I safe here in your world?"

"There are also safe places here as there are dangerous ones. You just have to avoid the troubled places."

"Your world is full of troubled places. If there are thunderstorms here, there are wildfires there. If there are tornadoes in this end, there's earthquake in the other end not to mention that in your world people are killing each other."

"It's a sad thing but it's true. Okay, Loro, as seeing is believing, I might come to see your world one of these days. Did you say that I just have to think of it to reach it?"

"That's right, Master. Even if you're not with a zobus, think of it to see it but, by the way, you've to say the magic word."

Rebmun stopped his inquisitions. The more the boy became suspicious. It came to him that the bird was only inventing stories – impossible stories that are hard for him to believe in.

IV

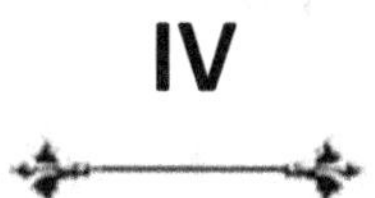

Classes were about to end; the summer vacation that Rebmun was excited about was fast coming.

"As both of you know, I'll be away for a week, but don't worry," Rebmun told his pets. "Somebody will be taking care of you while I and my parents are on vacation . . ."

"May I interrupt, Master . . . there's something I'd like to request," said the bird.

"Then say it."

"Can you free me from this cage while you're away? I'd like to visit the *Field of Pines* to see what my sister had been doing."

"What sister?" Rebmun asked in his suspicion the bird was about to make another issue. "You have a sister in the *Field of Pines*?"

"I left her accidentally during Varcoba's assault. I thought she died there that day but this morning I got her message in the wind saying she's in prison and due for execution next full moon unless I surrender to Varcoba the talisman of Yorka."

"What's your point?"

"Actually, I couldn't do it for a day so that I'm asking you to grant me temporary freedom. I need to go back to the Kingdom of Dome to rescue my sister."

"I'd be grounded if I lose you. Do you know how much my father spent to bail you out of Patrick's?"

"I don't need to know. What I need is for you to free me, and by the way, not only for a day and you must have to come with me too in case I need you to help me. I'll pay you. I have a box of gold hidden in a bunker."

"A box of gold?" Rebmun asked and laughed sarcastically. You never run out of tall tales, Loro."

"I'll give you half of it."

"Even if you give me all the gold you have, I still can't go. I'm running out of time."

"Find a way. Tell your parents you're going hunting with me before you go for vacation."

"Dad won't let me and I don't want to go against his will. You know, Loro, my Dad has this thing his doctor called 'high blood'."

"And how is it related to my request?"

"My Dad easily gets upset especially when he forgets to take his medicine. Also, he's suffering from stress. He'll be having chest pains. Then he feels like it's hard for him to breath. Then he has this severe headache and then comes dizziness. My father is very sickly, Loro, so I avoid upsetting him."

"You're a good son, but I, too, is a good brother. I must have to help my sister. Come with me even just for a day. Your parents won't know it."

"I'm sorry; it isn't me you need. My parents and I are going for a trip this summer. I don't have time to help you here."

"Can't you spare a day for me? For a day?"

"I don't think it would take only for a day if I go to your place. Am I safe if I go there?"

"No one can harm you there as long as I have the amulet with me. All you have to do is watch my back just in case . . ."

"That would put me in jeopardy."

"I thought we're buddies."

"It depends on the situation."

"Then you're not a true friend."

"Whatever you think, I'm not going."

"This is one help that I beg you. I won't be asking for another favor but this and forever, I'll be indebted to you."

"If I go and we fail in this mission, who will come to rescue us?"

"Humans can enter the Dome by saying the magic word and stay safe there as long as you utter the magic word now and then."

"I don't even know what the word is."

"I'll tell you the magic word if you're going with me. Then, if you want to come home, just say the same and you'd be back here."

"That's too weird for me to believe. Anyway, what's the magic word, abracadabra?" Rebmun asked and laughed.

Loro thought that the boy was just making fun of what he said. Yet, he revealed the magic word. Rebmun repeated it: "ZAYEXIWOVU."

"That's all you have to say and presto! You become invisible to the eyes of evil forces."

"But I didn't turn invisible when I said it?"

"It's because you said it plainly and you weren't requesting for anything."

"Requesting like what . . .?"

"If you request for something, say the magic word but remember that the power won't last long. It's gone after a minute and you have to say it again. Also remember to keep it a secret."

"What if Yorka just lied about it . . ."

"Yorka never lied."

"How do you know?"

"Yorka hadn't spoken lies in all his entire life according to the old denizens."

Rebmun had second thoughts about what the bird was saying. It sounded too impossible to be true. No doubts, Loro was lying!

"Are you coming with me or not?"

Convinced that Loro was only inventing stories, Rebmun bluntly answered, "No!"

"Would you rather want me to forget about my sister? You don't feel what I do, not what I do because you don't have any sister."

Even how much the lorikeet pleaded for him to listen, the boy was adamant. Rebmun walked towards the door to avoid discussing further nonsense things with the bird, but before he could hold the knob, the bird's screechy voice jolted him.

"They're here! They're here! Varcoba is here with her thirteen guzzlers. I saw them pass by just now! They know where I am! Don't open the door. Please, don't!"

The boy didn't believe what Loro said. Nevertheless, he placed an ear against the panel to listen what was coming up. A loud knock on the door startled him.

"That's them! Don't open, Master! They're here to get me."

"Who's there?" Rebmun yelled.

"It's me, son" Reba answered. "Your dad and I are going out and might be coming back late. Anyway, your nanny is here with you."

Embarrassed, the bird fell silent. In a little while, the boy went to bed. The dog lay down in his bed in one corner nearest to Rebmun's.

The night passed by with the boy and his pet bird harboring anger at each other.

The next day was a Saturday but the bird was screaming out the time when the clock struck six.

The boy refused to get out of bed. Annoyingly, the bird counted the numbers.

"Stop it! No school today, moron."

Yet, with a voice getting raspy, Loro kept on counting numbers.

Later that day, Rebmun asked his mother to take the cage out of his room. Reba promised to take out the birdcage to the porch starting the next weekend and until summer was over.

V

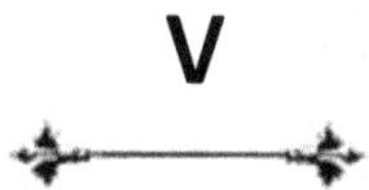

Loro's daily recitation of numbers had turned annoying to Rebmun. He thought of banishing the bird to the rainforest of Deervana that was home to thoroughly white sacred reindeers and exotic birds. It was thought of to be enchanted. Pets that ran away from their cruel masters sought sanctuary in this forest but they never returned home anymore.

Summer vacation started the next Friday evening. Rebmun felt relaxed with the thought that he could have all his time sleeping without the bird to wake him up in the morning.

"Goodnight, Loro," the boy scoffed. "Hope not to see you there when I wake up in the morning. You'll spend your nights at the porch, Mr. Squeaky and you'll be all alone outside throughout the night all summer through. What a laugh, ha, ha, ha!"

"Well, let's find it out tomorrow," the parrot whispered to his self. "We'll see it; we'll see it," the bird murmured.

The boy climbed to his bed, covered himself with blanket and went to sleep confident that his Mom would take the cage out of his room.

Unfortunately to Rebmun, his mother forgot to move out the bird that Friday evening and so, early the next morning, he woke up again to the shrill voice of the parrot.

"It's six O'clock! It's six O'clock!"

"Shut up!" the boy hollered, but the bird was determined to ruin Rebmun's day. He started screaming out the numbers. Even if the boy buried his head under a pillow he still could hear Loro's counting loud and clear. ***I must throw him out of the window,*** the boy thought. ***I must!***

"I told you to stop! Stop it!"

However, the bird continued counting.

"Shut up or I'll throw you out of the window!"

Yet the bird ignored his master's warning. He continued counting in his loud shrill voice until he made his master's blood boil. After mentioning the number 99, Rebmun got out of his bed and nearer to the cage, he yelled at the bird.

"Stop there! Stop it right now! The next time you mention a number, you'll find yourself outside!"

The bird held his breath wondering if his master was serious with his warning.

The boy, on realizing that the bird had his fear, calmly turned around to go back to sleep when all of a sudden, the bird shouted with all his might the next number.

"One Hundred!"

Rebmun turned around, opened the cage, grabbed the bird's feet, gripped them tightly and pulled Loro out of his cage.

"Wait, wait, wait . . . what are you doing?"

The boy ignored the bird. He opened the window.

"Are you throwing me out?"

"What do you think, smarty?"

"Don't. Please don't throw me out! It's not safe out there! Varcoba is here in the village looking for me."

"You deserve it! You deserve it!"

"I beg of you, Master Six O'clock," the bird pleaded for mercy but the boy was in his rage.

"You've gone too abusive!"

"Put me back, dimwit! If Varcoba finds me, she'll kill me! She'd surely kill me!"

"There's no Varcoba, no guzzlers, no Yorka and you have no sister left there in the field of pines. They're all in your dreams."

"Varcoba is real. Believe me!'"

"You made it up. Those were all products of your wrong imaginations. You were hallucinating."

"I won't force you to believe, but please don't throw me out! Have mercy, Master Six O'clock. Return me to the cage."

"You need to learn your lesson! Feed yourself and find a place to sleep tonight. Come back the next day if you're still alive!"

Once more, the bird asked for mercy but Rebmun was firm with his decision. He thrusted the bird outside the window and with all his might, the boy threw out the bird into the open air.

Once released from Rebmun's hold, the bird gleefully flapped his wings in the air and laughed to the boy's surprise.

"Geeee I'm free!" Loro screamed joyfully. "I'm free to fly again! I can eat fresh wild fruits again!

I'm having fun again!" Looking at Rebmun peeping through the window, the bird chuckled: "Best of all I can rest from counting numbers to wake up a sleepy, silly, stupid slugabed!"

The boy's jaw dropped on realizing the bird was able to manipulate him. The bird was free and there was no way that it would come back to his cage.

VI

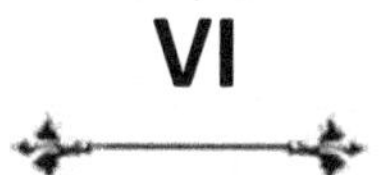

Away to freedom, the parrot flew. Rebmun thought it was heading to the forest of Deervana. Miles, who had witnessed the wrangle between his master and Loro could only whine as he watched the bird fly. In the next moments, the bird disappeared from his sight.

The boy hated what he did, could hardly believe he was outsmarted by a tiny-headed bird who had flown straight to the forest. He stared at it until it disappeared from his sight. He looked back at the open birdcage regretting of what he'd done. For a moment, he threw his eyes at the empty space where Loro had gone. *What if Varcoba and her guzzlers really exist and are looking for the bird in the forest of Deervana?*

Even the next day the boy couldn't stop thinking about his lost pet. *How was Loro doing during the rain? Did he find shelter? Did he find food throughout the day?*

Rebmun spent most of his time that day worrying about Loro and hoping to see the bird flying back home, but the bird was now nowhere to be seen. Rebmun's hopes drained down when twilight came without any sign of Loro's return.

Rebmun's parents learned that the bird was gone. They investigated their son and the boy made up his story that Loro found a way to slip out of the cage and flew away but he couldn't explain how the bird got out from his cage by himself.

"You threw out the bird outside because you were mad at him for waking you up in the morning," Newton Reed told his son outright which the boy wasn't able to dispute.

"He was upsetting me," said the boy.

"In many times I have told you not to make hasty decisions when not in the right mood to avoid doing wrong. You forgot about it again."

"Sorry, Dad I lost my temper."

"And you thought that you no longer need his coaching in counting numbers. I tell you, young man – you still need the drill."

"I already know how to count numbers."

"Not good enough. You forget sometimes. If the bird's not coming back . . ."

"He'll be coming back . . ."

"If he hadn't until the next Saturday, boy, you'll be grounded and you'll be ruining our plans for the summer."

Every day Rebmun kept watching for the return of his pet bird but there never was a sign of its coming. He thought that what Loro told him about where he came from was really true and the boy was worried that the bird might have gone back to the *Field of Pines* to rescue his sister from the hands of the evil specter the bird called Varcoba.

VII

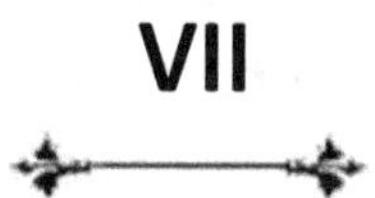

Loro hadn't returned home even after six days. Sometimes it came to Rebmun that the bird might really have gone back to the *Field of Pines* for his sister. On his second thought, Loro won't be doing it; he was aware that the evil Varcoba was there waiting for him. Whichever it was, Loro was in danger. Seeking sanctuary in the forest of Deervana couldn't be safe.

That Friday evening after supper, Newton and Reba Reed talked about the impossibility of Loro's return. They were discussing stories about those runaway pets who sought refuge in the forest of Deervana and never had returned.

Not wanting to hear the discussion, Rebmun went to his room. He took a look outside the window hoping to see a sign of Loro's coming. All that the boy saw there was the beauty of the night. The sky was filled with stars. The radiance of the full moon that seemed hanging a little bit over the top of the forest made the summer atmosphere look cool.

The boy lay down on his bed thinking about Loro: *where could he be by that time? Where did he get his supper? Where could he find a safe and cozy place to pass the night?* He remembered Loro telling him about the sister the bird accidentally left behind.

Rebmun wondered what the Field of Pines look like. Then in a little while, he lost consciousness. Then came a kind of dream he never have dreamed before.

In his dream, the boy was seeing the forest of Deervana. He saw Loro flying over a canopy of trees searching for a place where to rest. It was beautiful to sleep under the bright full moon at the top of a tree that sways like a hammock with the soft blow ing of the wind that could easily lure him to sleep. The breeze was cool and soothing that would keep him in slumber throughout the night.

Rebmun's dream went on.

Loro, made one more round over the trees. Finding a perch that could be a good place to spend the night, Loro alighted on a horizontal branch and confident of his safety, soon he had gone to a deep dreamless sleep.

But then, way past midnight, the parrot was awakened by the sound of huge wings flapping in the air. A giant hawk hovering way over the top met his eyes. Loro hunched that the giant hawk was there for him; he didn't make a move.

The lorikeet thought his life was in clear danger but he had no time to escape. The hawk had found him, ready to snatch him at any time he tried to move. No way that it would let this chance pass by.

"The evil woman would never rest until she gets the amulet."

Rebmun thought that Loro needs to fool the hawk with a trick by pretending he was unaware of the hawk's presence.

The Lorikeet closed his eyes tightly but kept on listening to the faint sound the hawk was making – the flapping of his wings. Then, as Loro intuited it, the hawk swiftly plunged straight down to where he was but the bird let himself fall down before the giant hawk could grasp him. He bounced in the branches of the trees and hit the ground over a thick pile of dried leaves.

Unharmed, Loro rose to his feet and found shelter under the thick bushes that concealed him from the hawk's sight.

Over the trees, the hawk roved like a chopper searching where the lorikeet had gone.

In his dream, Rebmun kept an eye at Loro hiding under the bushes for a long while. Loro kept himself still while waiting for the big black bird to abandon the area.

The sky had turned dark. Thinking it was safe for him to go back to sleep, Loro climbed back to the treetops. The giant hawk was already gone. There was silence all around at the top of the forest.

The bird found a crest at the top of a pine tree at a good distance away from where he formerly settled; it could be a much safer place for him to rest on.

For a moment Loro listened to the sound of the night. Except for the soft humming of the gentle breeze, the night was in deep silence. Up in the sky, there were countless little stars hanging. Loro tried to count them but got amiss. He shifted his thoughts to the giant hawk. He could hardly believe how that hawk had found him that fast.

Rebmun's dream went on.

Confident that the giant hawk had completely abandoned the forest, the bird tried to fall back to a good sleep.

From behind the dark clouds over the western horizon, the moon reappeared. That brightened the sky again. The bird felt relieved on the thought that soon it would be morning. Daytime in the forest was safer than nighttime.

Loro had closed his eyes and was about to fall unconsciousness when suddenly the hawk emerged behind his back. Too late to be aware of what's going to happen, the big black bird had grabbed the lorikeet's neck.

VIII

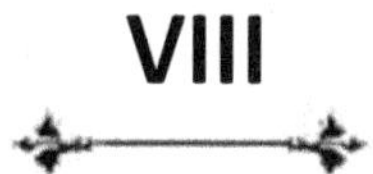

As swift as the wind, the hawk flew back to where he came from clutching Loro in his claws. Rebmun followed the hawk over mountains, valleys and rivers with his eyes fixed at the hawk's tail lest he might lose it from his sight.

Rebmun saw in his dream the coming of the morning. At the eastern horizon, daylights were creeping. The hawk glided in the wind. Then in a moment Rebmun noticed a thick field of evergreen trees beneath. He presumed it was the field of pines that Loro talked about.

In the next moment, the hawk was descending. On a huge rock fronting a hill of thick dark mist, the big black bird alighted. The boy thought it was the place that Loro called   the Kingdom of Dome, his home which the evil Varcoba took by force.

As its claws touched the rock, the hawk magically transformed itself into a handsome black man with splendid build looking like a magnificent warrior. Loro was gone from Rebmun's sight but he assumed that the white young lad squatting beside the black man was the bird the hawk abducted. The young lad was in his teens, slim and fair-skinned with a rainbow-colored hair. His multicolored pants and shirt in vivid green reminded Rebmun of Loro's multicolored feathers.

In a little while the thick dark mist dissipated and a huge dome made of gray stone came into Rebmun's view which could be the entrance to the Kingdom of Dome that the bird had been talking about.

A door opened and the black young man entered dragging the poor kid beside him. The door closed back.

By this time, Rebmun had entered into his dream, finding himself right at the doorstep of the Dome. He tried to step into the door but he couldn't move.

Loro's in danger; I've got to rescue him. I have to come inside but I can't move my feet. I need to say the magic word. ZAVUYEXIWO, LET ME COME INSIDE.

The door didn't open. He must have said it wrong. Rebmun recollected it was a word of ten letters but misstated it. The boy tried to jumble the letters in his mind. He found it.

ZAYEXIWOVU! PLEASE LET ME IN!

The door opened slowly slightly enough for the boy to get in. It closed automatically behind him. One of the guards looked back on suspicion that somebody had come in. The boy immediately hid himself behind a big pillar.

Rebmun took a glance at the center of the hall. There was a small crowd gathering there. Everybody's attention was on the elevated platform where sat an old ugly woman on a grandiose furniture that looked like a chair intended for a queen.

Rebmun thought that the ugly woman could be the Varcoba that Loro talked about. Her face was thin and wrinkled. Her brows were thick and as black as her monstrous eyes. Her nose was thin and long and as pointed as her chin that almost touched her flat chest. Her lips were also thin and dark but her mouth was wide. She wore a loose solid black dress with its hem reaching her ankles; the sleeves were touching her wrists. With her long black nails, her fingers were elongated and thin. The boy thought they were but skeletons. To Rebmun, the old woman was a perfect picture of the witches in the books of fairy tales except that she was not wearing a black hat that would have partly covered her long black hair.

The ugly creature sniffed and stood up.

As quickly as the ugly woman stood up, Rebmun moved back behind the post. His heart was beating fast for he thought that Varcoba had noticed him.

"I smell something strange around here," Varcoba spoke; her voice was as shrilly as Loro's. "An alien had come inside. He's here with us."

"Probably, it's the zobus that Dargo brought," a guard responded.

Varcoba shifted her eyes to the young lad standing beside Dargo.

"Dargo, I'd like to believe this is the evasive Poutric?" Varcoba told the black muscled man.

"You're right, my Lady," Dargo replied. "Our search for the amulet is coming to end."

"Splendid, Dargo, splendid," Varcoba said clapping her hands in appreciation of what Dargo did. "I know I can always rely on you."

"I feel honored, dear Varcoba."

The evil woman clapped her hands again calling everybody's attention.

"Let it be known throughout this kingdom that this zobus, Dargo is slated for promotion to the rank of a captain in the next full moon."

The crowd roared their protest.

"Nobody here has the right to go against my wishes. My decision is final!"

"Thanks, Varcoba," Dargo responded in appreciation to the old lady's announcement.

Dargo pushed Poutric onward. The boy stumbled to the floor; his lips touched Varcoba's long lean feet which made her think the young lad was totally yielding the Kingdom of Dome to her power.

"Welcome back, Poutric. How have you been? You returned at the right time to witness the execution of your sister."

The lad rose up in anger.

"Mimosa has nothing to do with my escape. You're persecuting the wrong person."

"Yet your sister has to pay for your mistake. You forgot the law in the Field of Pines."

"Now that I came back, release my sister!"

"Not that fast, my boy. First of all show to me the amulet of the Dome."

"I don't know what you're talking about."

"The talisman of Yorka, don't you know about it?" Varcoba seemed upset. "Like all the other zo-buses, you're a liar," Varcoba raged.

"Be careful with your words," Poutric warned. The crowd roared. Varcoba grimaced.

"Well, I like liars. They'd keep me good company. Now, for the last time, Poutric, where's the amulet?"

"Why do you keep asking? If I'm a liar, do you expect me to tell the truth?" Poutric dauntlessly reacted.

"You will for the freedom of your sister!" Varcoba replied harshly and commanded a guard, "Bring to me the prisoner Mimosa!"

On Varcoba's command, a guard left the hall and came back in a few minutes dragging behind him a huge cage. Inside was a pretty young girl older than Poutric. She was still wearing the same royal ensemble she wore when Varcoba attacked. It was a white garment now tattered and soiled, frilled with yellow and pink laces that stretched down to her heels. Like Poutric, she had a rainbow-colored hair, straight and silky. Her eyes were as green as Poutric's; her lips were as red as strawberries; her cheeks were creamy pink like her brother's, her pointed nose was a little bit upturned.

Mimosa's face brightened up on seeing Poutric. It was their first time seeing each other since his sudden escape from the Field of Pines some full moons ago.

The guard opened the cage releasing the former princess of the Kingdom of Dome. She ran to her brother and gave him a hug.

"I apologize for not holding you tightly when I escaped," Poutric whispered.

"You were turned into a bird and I was too heavy for you to carry, so I released myself from holding you. Why did you come back when you were already free out there?"

"I wasn't free at all. I was also held in a cage, but not a captive. Through the whispers of the wind, I came to know that Varcoba is holding you and had sentenced you with execution. Now, that I'm here, I mustn't leave without you."

"That is such a touching reunion, but enough of it," Varcoba interrupted. Her shrill angry voice caught the attention of the siblings. "Look at your sister, Poutric. Is it not a waste if I roast her under the sizzling sun at the apex of the Dome? I must tell you that before your sister gets sundried, she'd be feasted by my hungry guzzlers until nothing is left of her but her dried bones. Well, I changed my mind."

Delighted and anticipating for a good riddance, the siblings looked at Varcoba.

For a while, the old ugly woman stared at the royal children who were eagerly waiting for her to say something.

"I'd give you the chance to save yourselves, wastrels!" Varcoba said. "Think about it."

Rebmun's dream went on.

IX

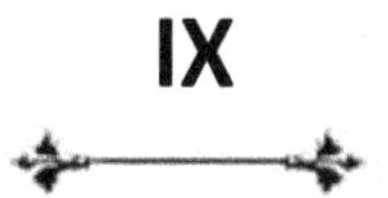

Varcoba clapped her fragile hands once more. On the doorway to the hall there emerged another guard dragging another huge cage that had inside it a young white man as tall and as splendid as Dargo.

"Here's another fool who needs no introduction."

"Rafos!" Poutric gasped. The lad never thought the captain of the kingdom's high-level troop was still alive. The last time he saw Rafos, was when he fled. He saw the loyalty of the man fighting alone against the thirteen guzzlers.

"Now, I'm confident. I believe we could get back the Kingdom of the Dome," Rafos whispered to Poutric who was at arm's length from him. "Let's just wait for a good chance."

"You surprised me, Rafos; All the while, I thought you were dead!"

"We lost our fight defending the Dome because this big cheater brought with her an army of a thousand demons and ghouls . . ."

"A thousand demons and ghouls . . . it's against the laws of war as agreed upon by the leaders of the dark kingdoms."

"Not permissible per agreement of all the nations composing the dark world, but she's an incredible cheater. We were outnumbered and there was no way for us to match their strength and power. When you were gone, a huge number of zobuses lost their lives but I was able to escape."

"You escaped? Did you abandon your soldiers?"

"I fought until I was captured and thrown to prison. That was when I learned that Mimosa was also held captive. All I had in mind while I was in prison was how to rescue your sister. I won the trust of my prison guard whose name is Zacron. He helped me escape.

"I'm afraid that the prediction about our tribe getting extinct is coming true. Had the spirit of Yorka forsaken us?"

"Yorka's spirit can't help us; the amulet was gone from its place," Rafos replied. "I found some other zobuses who survived the battle. We grouped ourselves and made plans to attack Varcoba to free your sister. I only waited for a chance to retaliate."

Incidentally, Varcoba heard the last words of Rafos.

"You're a big fool! You can no longer reclaim the Kingdom of Dome. You need a hundred more of your kind to defeat even one demon."

"If you did not bring your demons and ghouls . . ." Poutric yelled back.

"Accept the truth, idiots. Your race is bound for extinction. You better advise all your surviving zobuses to disperse. And you, Rafos. Now you regret for refusing the once-in-a-lifetime deal I offered."

"What was the deal, Rafos?" Poutric asked in a whisper.

"She offered me to be the king of her empire," Rafos whispered back and chuckled. "But I have to sleep with her in my entire life."

"That's disgusting," Poutric scoffed.

"Hey, as much as I love to watch men gossiping, I need to cut in. Time is running out!"

"Goddess Varcoba, grant me the right to speak," Rafos said from his cage.

"Get it off."

"Spare the lives of the royal siblings."

"Not as easy as that . . ."

"In return, I'll join your force like what Dargo did. You need me to strengthen your power. With me and Dargo on your side, you'd conquer all the kingdoms in the dark world."

"What a splendid idea but I know pretty well that you're only trying to fool me. Do you think I'm dumb? I had been using that old trick." Varcoba said, laughed wildly and turned to the young lad: "As you know it, Poutric, this zobus here is your sister's ardent lover. He was the one who groomed you to be the royal guardian of the Dome and that's what you should be as your inherent responsibility."

"So well. You know what was happening inside the kingdom," Mimosa butted in.

"Pretty well. If you tell Poutric to hand me the amulet of Yorka, I'll be leaving this Kingdom of Dome and never bother this place again."

"After all the destructions you did to us," Rafos yelled. "We're not as foolish as you are."

"Look who's stupid!" Varcoba screamed at Rafos with eyes turning deep red due to intense anger. "By the way, Poutric, this one tried to rescue your sister, but he ran out of luck and ended up in the cage that was reserved for you," Varcoba said. "You ought to thank him for taking the place that could have been yours."

"Is Rafos slated for execution?"

"That remains to be seen."

"How about Mimosa?"

"Her life is resting in your hand, Poutric."

Varcoba left outright leaving the prisoners in the care of her guards and guzzlers posted around the hall. She was about to exit when Rafos reminded her of the deal he offered.

"I won't be making any more good deal, Varcoba. Think about it."

"I have my soon-to-be ordained keeper of the Dome and captain of all my guards and the guzzlers. I believe he has your skill ten times better."

"And that's the zobus who betrayed Yorka and the entire Kingdom of the Dome. Dargo is no better than me. Why don't you pit his skill against mine to prove who between us is the better warrior?"

Varcoba clapped her hands and said, "That's a good idea! If that's what you want, my dear Rafos, your wish is granted. When do you want this duel to happen?"

"Right this moment; time is an important element," inferred the dauntless Rafos who was ever confident on himself in using weaponry. He won't be known as the great defender of the kingdom if he lacked the skill.

"Choose your weapon," Varcoba told Rafos after a guard released him from his cell.

"Whatever Dargo has."

"I assume you're ready for this fight, Dargo. Show me what this cocky guardian of the Dome is up to."

"Leave it to me, my dear Varcoba."

The two warriors readied themselves and took each other's stance.

"Don't fail me, Dargo. Don't ruin the trust that I have given you. My destiny to conquer the Dome is resting in your hands."

"On this very day, Varcoba, I'll let Rafos rest in peace", the cocky Dargo declared. "Poutric's good in counting. Let him count numbers. I promise you that before Poutric could count halfway to one hundred, Rafos will suffer the fate of Yorka and nobody among the zobuses will ever bother you again."

"Amazing, Dargo, amazing!" Varcoba applauded and freed a hellish kind of laughter. "Let the duel begin!"

All the while Rebmun kept watching his dream.

X

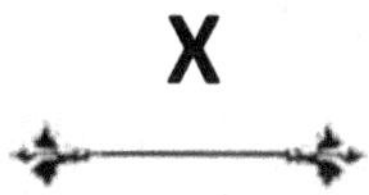

Rebmun sprinted to the bigger pillar while the guards and the guzzlers were busy watching Rafos and Dargo readying for the duel.

The two warriors were brandishing each other's weapon. In the face of Dargo was a trace of intense hatred; in the figure of Rafos was complete composure but both were staring at each other fiercely like two hungry beasts in the wilderness who were up to end each other's fate. Yorka trained both of them with the skill in using all the kinds of weaponry to be the best warriors in the kingdom. Now they're to pit against each other with their strength and skills; each one was confident to have mastered what Yorka, the former greatest warrior of the king

-dom had taught them; each one bore the confidence to outfight each other.

"At last, Rafos, I'd been waiting for this."

"It baffles me why you choose to be a foe when you had a better life in this kingdom."

"Let's call it plain envy."

"We were best of friends when we were young. We're like brothers, Dargo, and between us, envy shouldn't exist," said Rafos.

"Yes, we grew up together but you always had the edge over me. You won the trust of Yorka. You won the heart of Mimosa and reaped praises from the royal family and from all the zobuses. You grabbed all and left nothing for me when we were best of friends."

"We have the same desires and got the same chances. If you only told me about what you were up to, I should've given in to you in Yorka's name for I knew that he regarded you as his son."

"You knew it very well but you always wanted to prove to Mimosa that you were the hero, the pride of the kingdom, the high and the mighty that was worthy of her attention while I was always the weaker one."

"Don't get me wrong, my friend; I was always there for you."

"It was me who was always there for you. I was at your side in defending the royal throne when it was once attacked by one of the kingdoms of the Dark World. In many times I saved your life yet nobody recognized that not even you. You were always the focus of everybody's attention while I was but a mere dark figure moving under your shadow."

"I only did what I need to do," said Rafos. "I didn't have intentions to put you down for I treated you as a brother."

"You were too competitive at my expense."

"I didn't know what you were up to. I didn't mean to hurt you, Dargo. All I thought was to make you proud of me being your friend."

"But what you did was pain to me. Now comes the time that I will prove you cannot beat me in the use of weaponry. I'm a better warrior than you are, Rafos. In fact, I'm the best now of all the zobuses."

"Because of what you did many zobuses lost their lives. There are only a few zobuses left all because of the traitor that you are. You betrayed your own tribe."

"You made a traitor out of me!"

"You're darned wrong!"

"You caused me to betray our ancestors. You alone got the honor when I was fighting with you against the invaders. You're greedy of love and praises. What had become of me is your entire fault, Rafos. You're not worthy at all to be regarded a hero."

"If that's what you think in spite of my effort to save the Dome, I cannot do anything better to calm you down," said Rafos.

"I had been waiting for this showdown."

"My suspicion was strong. You desired to possess the amulet for glory and power. Now it's confirmed that you're one hell of a traitor! You were the one who killed Yorka in your desire to own the amulet of the Dome."

"Now that you know it, what can you do?"

"Enough!" Varcoba interrupted. "I don't need warring of words, ladies, I want action!"

Both warriors were at each other's stance. Varcoba was about to count down from three when she sensed a stranger was watching. She paused, her nose flaring and moved her head back and forth with her eyes glaring at every direction. She must not be wrong.

"Someone from the outside world is watching us," Varcoba hollered.

Rafos and Dargo momentarily distanced from each other on the command of Varcoba. She looked around in search of the intruder; her eyes roving like strobe lights.

"I was right! Somebody's snooping! Somebody had sneaked in! I can smell him. I can hear him breathe. Find this spectator!" Varcoba screamed at the guards.

XI

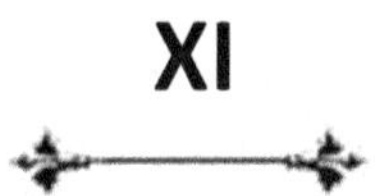

Rebmun was aware he was in danger. Once cap-tured the chance to escape could be too slim. From Loro, he learned that this devil's advocate was as mean as the lord from hell.

After a thorough searching and no one had found any intrusion, a guard called Varcoba's attention and dared to speak:

"Goddess Varcoba, I fear you're having again your hallucinations. I had inspected all the remote areas all over the hall and I am sure that no foreign element had intruded here."

"It's a human boy! I can smell him. I could hear him breathing. I could feel the heat from his eyes! I couldn't be wrong!"

"As I said, it's your hallucinations, Varcoba. I can prove that you are wrong," the same guard voiced out. "In fact, you'd been wrong for so many times."

"How dare you to insult me! What's your name?"

"It's Zacron."

"Well, Zacron, you committed a huge mistake against me for I'm not soliciting your opinion."

"You have to admit, Varcoba that at your age you can no longer depend on yourself. You're old enough to be our ruler."

"With one more blunder, I will banish you from here!" Varcoba snared – her red eyes turned more monstrous and her thin nose flared; she was catching her breath.

The old woman dropped herself to her throne and ordered the obnoxious guard to help do the search. At the top of her lungs, she screamed once more: "Continue searching!"

All the guards and the guzzlers fell in chaos again like ants rushing out from a wrecked anthill.

"Varcoba could be referring to the boy who hated numbers. I asked him to help me." Poutric told Mimosa.

Rebmun saw what was happening all around. He could see Varcoba sitting on the queen's chair with her eyes roaming around watching the guards scampering all over the hall in search of the intruder. In the midst of the chaos, Rebmun overheard Mimosa telling Poutric to escape while the guards were busy in their search.

"Now that I'm back, Mimosa, I won't be leaving without you."

"But you have to go. Now is your chance to save yourself."

"Then, you have to leave with me."

"I cannot abandon the Kingdom of Dome, brother. This had been the homeland of our ancestors, and I'm not giving this up to Varcoba. I'd fight to save this legacy from our parents. I will fight to my last breath."

"I must have to fight too. Anyway, Six O'clock, my newfound friend is here to help us."

Rebmun heard the sibling's conversation. Poutric was banking on his help, but the boy felt he was in danger in the hands of Varcoba if her guards would find him. The old devil woman was all out to get him. Rebmun thought no one could help him this time, but himself. There was no way to escape from the eyes of the guzzlers but to say the magic word which he immediately did: "ZAYEXIWOVU! PLEASE HIDE ME NOW!"

Right after Rebmun mumbled the magic word, he felt that everything within his sight was turning around him like an eddy and he was shrinking slowly and constantly into the inner section of the pillar.

In a short while, the boy realized he could no longer do a slight move. It was too late to realize that he made a mistake again. He couldn't even move his lips to utter again the magic word; was completely frozen. He shouldn't have said the magic word. The timing was wrong. Now, he couldn't move nor talk, but still he heard Varcoba's voice ranting.

XII

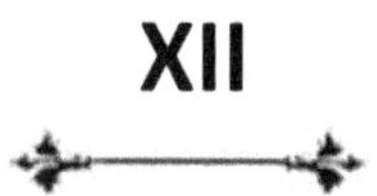

The boy could see the guards touching the posts one by one; they were coming near and that scared the boy for if the guards find him, he couldn't go back to his physical being anymore; he never would wake up again.

"Continue the search! I want to see the intruder!" Varcoba hollered. "He can just be around hiding behind the pillars! Touch every pillar you pass by. By doing that the pillar would turn transparent to your eyes. There's no way that the boy can hide inside it."

"You're just imagining things, Varcoba."

It was Zacron who spoke with his hands tied behind his back. The evil being cast a glowering look at Zacron's face but the guard stared back at her without a sign of fear.

"You again! How dare you to humiliate me!"

"Let's be honest to ourselves, Varcoba. Can it be that you're seeing things that are products of your imagination?"

"Shut up! How dare you to insult me!"

"It's time you have to admit you're too old to handle this risky job."

"I'm still capable to handle it; far more better than you are!"

"That's what you think, but the truth is you are physically handicapped. It's time to vacate your throne for the next-in-rank."

"And who could be that next-in-rank?"

"You forgot about me, Varcoba. I'm the most qualified among the guards."

"You can never assume the job I'm holding while I'm here. For humiliating me, you deserve five lashes! Guzzlers, you tie that good-for-nothing guard to a post," Varcoba ordered and freed out a horrifying wail that sounded like a cry of a banshee's. "Before the day's end, he must be gone from my sight!"

"Put back the prisoners to the cage," Dargo commanded the other guards. "Then continue looking for the intruder."

"Thank you, Dargo. I can always trust you." Addressing the guards, Varcoba announced, "My senses are telling me that the elusive outsider is hiding in one of these pillars. If the intruder is hiding there, at the touch of your hand, the post turns transparent; he can no longer hide from my eyes. That's the time we can grab him out from where he's hiding."

Rebmun could see the guards touching the posts one by one and they were coming near. That really scared the boy for if the guards find him, that would be his end. Rebmun realized he couldn't make a slight move like he was completely frozen; he couldn't move his lips to utter the magic word.

Rebmun was fully aware he was just dreaming. He heard Miles barking continuously from his room where his physical being was fast asleep. Waking up was the only way to escape from his nightmare. He thought of calling Miles but there wasn't a voice coming out from his mouth. If only his par ents would come to his room and wake him up, he wished.

Then came the knock on the door in Rebmun's room. It was Reba calling out the boy's name.

Reba wasn't able to come in. The door was locked

from inside and the dog couldn't open it by himself even if he tried to. All that Miles did was run around and bark hard to wake up his master. The dog failed.

Meanwhile, the guards continued touching the pillars. They had touched almost all the pillars around the hall except one – the post where Rebmun was hiding. The guards were coming nearer.

Inside Rebmun's room, Miles was still running around, barking for help. The boy was squirming in his sleep, groaning like he was desperately gasping for breath. Miles sensed he had to wake up his master. The dog was getting frantic.

Finally, on realizing there wasn't any help coming; the dog got up to the bed, bit the boy's pajama sleeve and exerted all his efforts to pull the boy down to the floor.

Rebmun's head had touched the edge of the bed. He was slowly sliding off, inches after inches, while his dream was going on. Miles exerted more strength. With the dog's final pull, the boy fell, banging his head, down to the carpet floor.

Rebmun's dream was over. The boy woke up a second before a guard had touched the pillar where he was hiding.

The boy was released from a fatal nightmare. With Miles licking his face, Rebmun got back to his senses.

XIII

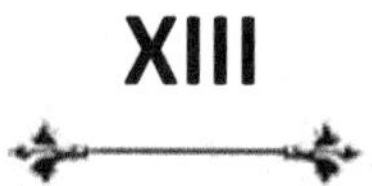

Rebmun was now into believing there was some truthfulness of what the bird told him, but didn't believe all what the bird said.

At the seventh day since Loro left his cage, Rebmun decided to go to the forest to rescue the bird believing that the evil forces of the dark world were there holding the bird in contempt. *If dreams do come true, then Loro was in danger; he needed help,* Rebmun thought.

Without his parents' knowledge, the boy slipped out through the window in his room immediately after lunch. With a backpack filled with things he and Miles needed for the day, Rebmun started his journey on a bike towards where the forest of Deervana loomed with Miles running after him.

After more than an hour, the boy and the dog reached an entrance to the interior of the forest. Under a thick bush, the boy hid his bike.

Rebmun trekked his way up through bushes and trees by foot with Miles following closely. It was the boy's first journey inside a forest and he felt greatly amazed on finding that the forest after all was quiet and peaceful. Rebmun didn't feel any danger lurking inside as he thought. He didn't see any other animals roaming around except for the two squirrels which were playing up and down the trees stirring the dried leaves and twigs on the ground. There were flowers of varied colors that spring had left to wilt in summer. It seemed the interior of the forest was a nice place to live in. No wonder that pets who had fled here as their sanctuary from wicked masters never returned home anymore. *But where are they?* Rebmun asked himself.

Rebmun and Miles walked on. As the boy was finding his way, he kept on shouting the bird's name every now and then and stopped to listen for a bird's call. He heard no response but the rustles of the leaves as the wind passed by.

The two were following a thin trail that seemed to end nowhere. When they seemed to have reached the midst of the forest, Rebmun saw a white deer down at the foot of the hill; his first time to see a thoroughly white deer.

He walked nearer to the deer; it was drooping beneath an old apple tree where strewed a number of red and green apples. The boy realized it was a doe and she was weeping; the boy heard her sniffling.

"Excuse me. May I know why are you crying?" Rebmun asked gently.

The doe lifted her head and stared at the boy for a few seconds. She drooped back without responding.

"I'm just trying to be friendly here. Maybe, I can help if you'd tell me why you're crying."

The doe looked at the boy once again and mumbled words to the boy's great surprise; the doe could talk well like Loro.

"Look at yourself. You're just a small boy. How can a small brain solve a problem that's as big as a mountain?"

"Don't judge me by my size."

"You could never be of help, little boy. Even if you have the guts to fight a foe, you don't have the strength."

"Try me."

"How sure are you of yourself? I don't want to cause a harm on you."

"You never know what I can do. Now, tell me what's your problem?"

"Don't you see what's happening? Look at the trees around you; they are dying."

It was then Rebmun noticed the surroundings. It looked different from the sceneries at the entrance of the forest. He saw no flowers and the trees were bare as if autumn had come again.

"What's happening here?" Rebmun asked.

According to the doe, the forest was affected with plague. Trees were under attack by armies of insects devouring the foliage, and even the barks and roots of the trees that animals could browse on.

"My empire is gone. I have lost all my companions and I'm in danger of losing my home. Now I'm dying of hunger for these fruits are uneatable; they're rotten with worms."

"My name's Rebmun. I come from the town of Moon Cap which lies at the foot of this hill. My parents live there."

"I'm Deervana, the owner of this forest. I inherited this from my parents who lost their lives when a severe storm ravaged this place many years ago.

If your town is right at the foot of this hill, it might be wiped out for there will be a flash flood if another heavy storm comes. To avoid the flood, we must save the trees from dying while we can."

"I can help you with that."

" What made you come up here?"

"I'm in search for my pet bird who flew away from home a week ago. He flew towards this direction. It might be that you've seen him and can tell me where to find him."

"But you have to help me first . . ."

"I will. Tell me how . . ."

"As you see, almost all the trees are dying. Millions of insects are constantly consuming the trees."

"I'm ready to help. Tell me what you need," Rebmun told the doe.

"We have to get rid of these insects, but we can't do it by ourselves," the doe said squaring her shoulders.

"Don't you know anybody who can help?"

"None could help us get rid of those insects, but the birds. We need the help of the birds but Tenten is holding them captives."

"Who's Tenten?" asked Rebmun.

"He's a bird-eating giant. He's staying in a cave that used to be my lair. It's in the center of this forest, the one nearest to a pond."

"Darn! Did you say Tenten is a bird-eating giant? My pet flew to this forest a week ago and had never come back since then. It's a lorikeet."

"The lorikeet!" Deervana gasped. "I saw the giant this morning with a lorikeet in hand returning to the cave. Tenten got your bird! Oh, he could have eaten the lorikeet for his lunch."

Rebmun drooped. He should have carried his plans a day earlier; he came too late.

The boy was about to give up hope seeing Loro alive when he heard the doe speak again.

"But I might be wrong! Tenten never eats parrots. He uses them as his rousers."

"How's that?"

"The giant sleeps during the day and the parrots would wake him up at six in the evening."

"But how do the parrots know the time?"

"I don't know. Maybe they know it by instinct. The giant would stay fully awake the whole night going around the forest to gather more birds sleeping on the trees. He returns to the cave before the sun rises up the following morning."

"So the giant came back to the cave late this morning with a lorikeet."

"Right," the doe responded right away.

"Is the giant a native to this forest?"

"No, I've never seen him before. A few full moons ago, he suddenly appeared here and made my home his living quarter. I was forced to move out."

"A while ago and you never have done anything to free the birds."

"How can an old deer topple a giant without anybody's help?"

"What was Tenten doing if he wasn't gathering birds?"

"First he fenced the entrance to the cave. Then he made cages out of woods, barks and made ropes out of the lily stems he gathered from the pond. He'd been gathering birds during the night for his food. It seemed he was searching around for a particular bird and I think it was your bird he'd been looking for. I saw him dance around the pond like celebrating when he found the lorikeet. In all those days the giant was working, he wasn't aware I was spying on him."

"How many birds are there in the cages?"

"There are ten cages hanging all over inside the cave and each cage has ten birds of the same kind. My constituents feared that if the giant runs out of birds to eat, he might consider eating other animals in sight so they migrated to the other forests for their own safety."

"Why did you not come with them?"

"I can't just leave this forest as easy as that. This has been my home and this is the only legacy my parents left me."

"So you don't surrender this rainforest without giving a good fight."

"You're right," Deervana replied. "And I need someone to fight with me."

That's where you need me."

"But you're just as big as I am. You can't topple a giant. Remember that he's huge and strong and sturdy."

"We'll fight him not by force but by brains," Rebmun responded. The doe didn't get what the boy meant. She stood still analyzing until the boy spoke again. "So where did Tenten come from and how did you know his name?"

"Nobody knew the giant's real name. He might have come from a newly-established colony which is about ten mountains and ten rivers away from here."

"So, that's how he got his name . . ."

"I referred him as Tenten because he consumes ten birds daily. He always had no less than a hundred birds in the cages and that's good for ten days. He gathers birds during the night when he roamed around the forest and also gathers food for his captives."

"Our mission now is to free the birds. They can help us get rid of the insects that are devouring the trees," Rebmun said.

"Exactly. Then we have to move now to reach the cave while the giant is still asleep," Deervana concluded while gazing at the afternoon sun. We have a good couple of hours to go before the clock strikes six tonight. If you follow me, guys, the cave is just beside the pond at the center of the forest."

XIV

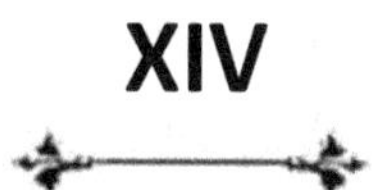

The boy and the dog followed Deervana. Pretty soon, Rebmun heard a faint roar.

"Did you hear that roar?" Rebmun asked. "Was that a lion?"

Deervana listened. She heard nothing.

"It could be the snore of Tenten. There are no lions here, no tigers, no bears, no wolves nor foxes. All I had here were peace-loving inhabitants until Tenten came. That drove them away," said Deervana.

"If that was Tenten's snore, then we're just very near to the cave," Rebmun commented.

"A stone's throw," Deervana replied.

"Is the giant still sleeping by this time?"

"Dead to the world, I'm pretty sure. Nothing could wake him up but the parrots in the cage and that would be at six O'clock in the evening. Meanwhile, we're safe."

"In that case, we can rescue my bird easily."

"Probably will, but oh . . . how can we get inside the cave?" Deervana said and mused. "Remember that Tenten fenced the entrance and secures the door with a lock and key before he goes to sleep."

"That's when we have to use our brains. We must find the key."

"Yes, the key . . . where does he hide the key?" Deervana murmured.

"Think. Think," said Rebmun.

"I'm thinking," Deervana said sounding upset. The doe closed her eyes tightly, squeezing her memory. Suddenly, her face brightened up.

"Yes! I know where the key is!" the doe blurted. "Once when I snooped around here, I noticed the giant preparing to sleep. I saw him putting the key inside his mouth. The giant sleeps at the bank of the pond with the key inside his mouth."

"Now we know where he keeps the key to the door of the cave and at this time he's sleeping and nobody could wake the giant up except the parrots."

"Exactly, but how could we get it?" Deervana asked.

"Easy!" Rebmun responded in a split of a second. "The giant is probably sleeping on his back and breathing through his nose."

"Exactly!" the doe responded.

"He inhales a good volume of air and exhales the same."

"Exactly!" Deervana responded in the same tone without blinking an eye while waiting for the boy to say something again.

"If I clasp his nose right after he inhaled, he breathes out hard through his mouth the same volume of air he inhaled enough to toss a tiny key to the air."

"Splendid!" Deervana shouted and shushed herself at once. "What if he wakes up? What if we're making extra noise and . . ."

"Only the parrots could wake him up and at six O'clock yet. Are you sure of that?"

"Oh yes, on many times I witnessed it," concluded the deer.

"Then he wouldn't wake up until the hour of six

and in that case we still have lots of time to execute our plans."

"Exactly. We have to move now to reach the cave while the giant is still fast asleep."

Rebmun looked at his wrist watch and said, "We have about a couple of hours to go before the clock strikes six tonight."

"Right," the doe responded. "If you follow me, guys, the cave is just beside the pond at the center of the forest."

The three continued to move – slowly and vigilantly – down to the cave. Deervana was leading the way followed by Rebmun with his backpack. Miles was following them silently.

XV

The doe was about to come out of the woods right in front of the cave. She slowed down; one step after another. Rebmun and Miles did as well. They looked around and crouched, listening for any sound. They heard nothing, but the little rustles they made and the snore of Tenten who was now in their sight lying a few yards away from the mouth of the cave. Sizing him up, the boy thought the giant's physical appearance wasn't intimidating at all; just a little bigger than the biggest human he ever had seen.

"Hold it! Don't rush in," the doe warned Rebmun when she noticed the boy was about to sprint towards where Tenten was.

"Okay," the boy said in agreement and positioned himself like he was ready for a long-distance running race.

"To attack an enemy, you need to do it on the right time; so wait for my signal," the doe instructed.

Rebmun took a deep breath to muster up his guts. Before Deervana could signal him to go, Rebmun was on his way towards the sleeping giant.

"Stupid boy! Stupid!" Deervana was cussing Rebmun for not following her instruction.

As soon as the boy reached the sleeping giant, without wasting a moment, he sprung into the giant's forehead like mounting onto a horse's saddle placing the giant's head between his knees. The giant never woke up, anyway, even if the boy was sitting on his forehead.

The boy readied himself with his fingers interlocked to clip the giant's nose. He waited for a moment when the giant could have breathed in again a large volume of air. Deervana and Miles cautiously walked towards the lake while watching in fear what Rebmun could be doing next.

In the next moment, Tenten breathed in a huge volume of air. Then so quickly, Rebmun clipped the giant's nose with his clasped hands as tightly as he could before the giant could exhale. The giant freed out a loud snort. That scared Rebmun, but the more efforts the boy exerted in locking the giant's nose with his fingers. The giant hadn't waken up, but struggling to breathe out. At this moment, the dog positioned himself at the bank of the lake. The doe followed and settled herself not far from where Miles was.

Unconsciously, Tenten opened his big mouth and breathed out so hard tossing a tiny key into the air as Rebmun expected.

Miles figured out where the key was going. Into the pond the dog quickly jumped and readily swam towards the spot where the key was about to drop. The dog caught the key in his mouth before it could fell into the water.

"Good job, Miles! Good boy!" Rebmun said on seeing what Miles did. He jumped from the giant's head, and got the key from the dog's mouth. At these moments, the giant was still in deep sleep.

Gripping the tiny key in his hand, Rebmun rushed to the cave and opened the lock but before he could open the door, Loro saw the boy and out of surprise, the bird shouted.

"It's six O'clock! It's six O'clock!"

All the ten parrots in the cage repeated the words in chorus. It was Tenten's wakeup call and it occurred to Rebmun that might rouse up the giant from his sleep. Thinking he had no time anymore to open all the ten cages to free all the birds, he rushed back to the big stump to conceal himself from the eyes of the giant leaving the door to the cave open. He held his breath while shaking like a leaf for fear that the giant was about to wake up soon.

XVI

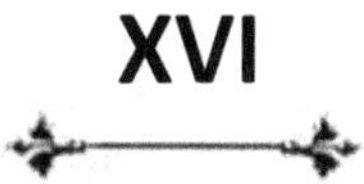

Rebmun had hidden himself behind a big stump not far from where the giant was. The doe and the dog were behind another stump. All the three of them watched in fear when Tenten opened his eyes. Gently, he stood up, stretched his robust body and yelled in a rough harsh voice.

"No use of hiding, trespassers!" Tenten sniffed; his nose flared. "No use of hiding for I know where you're hiding, I can smell your presence! Better come out now!"

The giant's roar made Rebmun shake more in fear. He thought of running away but his desire to save Loro and bring him home gave him more courage. He was already there and there was no other way but face the giant in a fair deal.

"Listen and listen carefully for I will not repeat this anymore. Show yourself! Now!"

After a moment of contemplation, the little boy decided to show himself to the giant. Slowly, he rose up from hiding. The giant's huge figure standing a couple of meters away from him, formed gradually before the boy's eyes. The giant was wearing a loin cloth made of animal skin just like the picture of typical cavemen the boy had seen in books. If not for his black thick brows and round bulging eyes, Rebmun thought the giant wouldn't look scary at all. He stood behind the stump but in full view of the giant.

"Interesting!" the giant spoke scrutinizing the size of the boy at the same time. "It's but a skunk!"

"I'm not a skunk!" Rebmun shouted back in his effort to hide his fear, yet the giant noticed it in his voice.

"What are you here for, silly brat?" Tenten asked in a loud tone and roared as loud as thunder, but it was how the giant addressed him that he got really scared. He clenched his teeth; his big blue eyes blinked unsteadily. The boy couldn't say a word but kept staring at the giant's face.

The doe and the dog moved out from behind the mound and quickly hid behind the stump close to where Rebmun stood before the giant could notice them.

"Don't show your fear," the doe whispered loudly. "That would add confidence to your opponent. Tell him you're not afraid of him."

"No need of shouting. I'm-not-afraid-of-you, Big Man!" Rebmun said trying to hide his fear. Yet the giant could tell that the boy was scared; his voice was faltering; his eyes, unsteadily blinking.

"Then . . . why are your hands trembling?"

The boy clenched his fingers to stop his hands from shaking. It took him a little while groping for an answer. Having mustered some guts, he shouted again, "My hands shake when I get mad, and it's you who is making me mad, Mr. Giant!"

"Oh, yeah . . .?" Tenten chuckled and looked around as if he was speaking before a wide crowd: "This little imp is mad at me." Looking down at the boy, he yelled with anger in his voice. "What are you mad at, squirrel?"

"You stole my pet bird . . ." the boy spontaneously reacted. He gazed straight into the giant's eyes.

"Stole is a wrong word. Revise! I gather birds from the trees; they got no owner!"

"I own the lorikeet you got this morning. I want you to release it!" Rebmun ordered explicitly to the amusement of the giant. He roared laughing like thunder.

"You scared me!" Tenten mocked. "Not as simple as that, Moron! What's the deal?"

"I'm not making any deal!"

"Well, shorty, I can't release my captives that easy. I worked hard to get all those birds. Mister Goblin, if you don't know it yet, then I'm telling you now that freedom is not free; you have to fight for it if you want it."

"I'm not listening to you anymore!" Rebmun shouted putting his hands on his hips. "Whether you like it or not, I demand you let my parrot go!"

"Oh, please don't scare me," the giant said and laughed while staring at the boy. Somehow, he admired the boy's tenacity.

"I'm serious with this: Free all the birds!"

"Okay," the giant said with raised hands. "I like dwarves with gigantic guts. I'll give you the bird; my reward to you for your courage to cross my territory, but on one condition."

"This is not your territory. You're just a trespasser here. It's Deervana who owns this as her inheritance. She has all the documents and by law, this forest belongs to her so you've got to leave this forest."

"Bwaaa ha ha ha! What law are you talking about, idiot? I am the law here and for all you know, Deervana doesn't have the rights to be a ruler of this forest because she isn't a good ruler in the first place. If she were, she wouldn't have abandoned her domain."

"Deervana never left. She's here and just waiting for the right moment to confront you."

"What do you want me to do, my Lord?" Tenten asked with sarcasm.

"Return Deervana's lair to her and release all the birds. This forest is dying and only the birds could bring its life back. But first, give me back my lorikeet."

"You mean your parrot. I have ten of them; they look all the same. Which one is yours?"

"I would take a look at them," Rebmun said and carefully made a few steps towards the cave. Through the bars, he saw various birds in cages. One cage which was hanging immediately next to the door was full of parrots; they were all identical. There were more other birds deep inside the cave, countless of them of different kinds and in different cages.

Deervana was right, Rebmun thought. There were countless of birds held in the cages and if he could free all of them, definitely, they could help in getting rid of the insects that were damaging the trees.

"Which one of you is Loro?" Rebmun asked.

"Me, Loro. Me, Loro," all ten parrots replied.

The boy asked again the same question and got the same answer. He looked back at the giant and shouted:

"I can't identify which one is Loro."

"Then I cannot release any of them," the giant replied, shouting back in a bold low tone.

"I got an idea," said the boy bouncing his right fist upward and ran nearer to the giant.

"Okay, what is it, Mr. Simpleton?"

"Release all the parrots; get them all out of the cages. The one that comes to me is surely the one I am looking for . . . Right?"

"Wrong! That doesn't make sense, dumb head!" yelled the giant, obviously mad because of the silly trick the boy tried to pull. He drew his face closer to Rebmun's, closer that the boy could smell his stinking breath. "Do you think you can outsmart me? Huh!"

XVII

The boy was caught off guard. His eyes swelled as he stared at the giant's face; so afraid the giant might suddenly whisk him with his tongue like how a frog does to a bug. He froze for seconds until he heard Deervana again.

"Fight your fears. You can beat him. Have confidence in yourself. You can beat him!"

"I can beat you!" Rebmun shouted at the giant out of reflex on the doe's motivation.

Tenten freed out a loud laughter.

"I'll take that as a challenge, street urchin. Prove to me how tough you are."

"I'm not a street urchin! Why do you keep calling me names? I hate it!"

"I call you names whenever I want to. You talk more than you can think, bro."

"Excuse me, I'm not your bro!"

"Oh, yeah, whatever."

"On the contrary, I can think better than you do. You may have a bigger head but you've nothing inside there but air like a ball," Rebmun said and laughed sarcastically so hard that upset his opponent.

"Shut up! I'm not wasting my time listening to your chat-chat. You're talking like a parrot."

"What?" All the ten parrots in the cage groaned in protest against Tenten's comments.

"That was an insult to us," a parrot commented. "He's looking down on us."

"The ogre's degrading us," another parrot voiced out its anger. "He thinks we are nonsense talkers! Although we're birds, we also have our freedom of speech!"

"I consider that as an oppression on our ability to express ourselves. He needs to know that we're not just ordinary birds. We're the smart ones," another expressed vehemence.

"Ssshhhh . . ." Loro shushed them. "We have to listen what's going on."

The giant continued his derision.

"You're talking nonsense like a parrot, midget! I will free your bird on one condition. As I told you, freedom is not free."

"Okay . . . calm down," Rebmun said trying to pacify the giant. "I challenge you to a game."

"Say your game now so we can have a deal! If I lose, I will give up all my captives to you and I will leave this forest for good with nothing. What's your bet?"

Rebmun stood still, rubbing his chin with his fingers. He looked around and all of a sudden pointed to the stump where the dog and the doe were hiding.

"I have my friends hiding there. You can have them for dinner tonight."

"That's a very stupid boy!" said the doe, jolted by what she heard. She came out from hiding. Miles followed the doe while barking in protest of what he heard.

"Gross!" Tenten said in disgust. "A yucky dog and a stinky deer! Is that all you can offer?"

"That's all I have."

"Holy Crap! I can't even stand the smell of a goat. I better starve."

"Then what do you want, picky old man?"

"What do you have aside from that trash?"

"Trash? Holy smoke! This forest is my kingdom!" Deervana squirmed in protest.

Tenten ignored her. His attention was at the boy who was intently staring at him.

The giant drew his face again closer to the boy. "Don't you have any other bet aside from that garbage?" Tenten asked.

"Well, I won't mind if you want to have me for your supper," Rebmun said squaring his shoulders.

"Yuck! I'm not a cannibal, Scaramouch."

"Then, what do you want, slow-thinker?"

"Just get your big mouth out of here if you lose. Got it? Now, name your game, silly boy!"

The boy responded in a snap; already had it in his mind.

"It's a race in counting numbers."

"What?" Loro's eyes swelled. "You'll lose sleepy, silly, stupid slugabed! You will lose!" the parrot shouted. Rebmun heard him.

"That's Loro! No need for the contest. I know it now which one is my bird!"

"Upppsss, the deal is closed," Tenten cut in.

"Rebmun," Deervana called from behind. "Remember that we got to free all the birds to save my forest from dying. That's mainly what we're here for."

"Okay, Mr. Giant, the race must go on."

"Good," the giant said. "I'll set the rules."

"Do as you wish right away! No dilly-dally. We have to finish this contest as soon as possible for I must be back home before sundown."

The giant shrugged his shoulders dismissing what the boy said. He sat on a big stone in front of Rebmun and held up his right hand, gesturing as if he had the authority to set up the rules. Everybody listened to the rules the giant imposed.

"I'm keeping a hundred birds in the cave. Let's start by counting numbers up. Whoever reaches first the hundredth number will have all the birds totaled in the last number he says."

"Shoot!" Rebmun immediately approved but in a matter of seconds voiced out his reluctance. "That sounds unfair. I'm just a dumb silly boy and you are an old smart big man who can even easily count all the stars in the sky on a starry night without amiss. We are not on an equal footing."

"You're complaining of what you picked. Make up your mind, silly brat!"

"No wonder you're calling me silly brat. Why don't you give this dumb head an edge over you to be fair, Mr. Wiseman?"

"What do you wish this time, fickle-minded?"

"We play the same game, but we'll have a change of rule," Rebmun said.

"What change of rule, Big Head? What change of rule? Make it clear!"

"We start at the same time as agreed upon but while I count from zero up, you do the reverse – from one hundred down and whoever finishes first wins."

The giant didn't agree instantly. He laid his eyes at the boy studying if the boy didn't set him up with a trick.

"I know that doesn't matter to a smart giant like you," Rebmun quickly added to what he proposed.

"Whatever rule you wish, simpleton, I'd never back out," the giant agreed.

Rebmun picked Deervana as the race moderator with Tenten's approval and the doe's assurance of fair deal.

The moderator arranged the setup. She required the two contestants to sit side by side facing her for easy watch.

"There will be no muffling of voices," said the doe. "No messing up. The numbers from zero to one hundred or the reverse as the case may be should be said clearly and accordingly. Any default would be ground for losing. Do you understand what I'm saying, gentlemen?"

The contestants agreed.

XVIII

All the birds inside the cages fell silent anxious-ly waiting for the doe to start the race. They were convinced that the boy was really smart and they were confident on the ability of the boy in counting numbers.

Loro, on the other hand, was afraid for Rebmun; he thought that the boy who hated numbers surely would lose. However, the bird realized how dearly he was to his master. The boy braved in crossing the enchanted forest to look for him and now he's trying to rescue him from the hands of Tenten.

"Are the contestants ready?" Deervana, the race moderator asked.

"Absolutely," Tenten replied quickly. Rebmun was staying silent - doubtful if he was doing the right thing. Loro on the other hand felt the same. He knew how dumb was the boy in counting numbers, but all the other birds were excited to watch the race of counting numbers between the boy and the giant.

The contestants were squatting on the ground at arm's length beside each other. The doe moved to the front of them. Once more, she clarified to the contestants the rule and procedure of the game. Once more, the contestants said in agreement.

Everybody was silent while waiting for Deervana's go signal. At her count of three, the race started.

Rebmun, saying the number loud and clear, sped up to the fifties while Tenten was slowing down to the seventies. The birds were listening intently. They hoped for the boy to win. Loro on the other hand remained silent; doubtful on Rebmun's ability to count numbers.

As the boy's number got higher, he was getting more tense. Then his counting turned slower as if it was hard for him to remember the next number to say. After number 89, Rebmun's mind shut off. The giant was counting slowly but continuously down while Rebmun kept saying number 89. Then the boy turned silent while Tenten went on with his counting.

"There you go, Mr. Cocky," Loro scoffed.

Afraid the boy was about to lose the race that could cost their freedom, the birds were hugging each other for comfort. Rebmun could only hope for the help of Loro, but the bird showed no concern at all; extremely upset at the boy's stupidity in choosing the number game. The giant had passed down to the twenties when Miles sprinted towards Loro and growled.

"It's ninety, sleepy-silly-stupid slugabed!" Loro angrily shouted after Miles had growled.

Rebmun caught what Loro shouted and sped up. He was able to finish his counting, but it was too late for him. A couple of seconds before the boy could say the one hundredth number, the giant had shouted "zero" to the dismay of the hundred birds inside the cave. The voice of Tenten mentioning "zero" froze all the birds inside the cages. In the ears of Rebmun it reechoed countless times making him looked wretched. There's no other way he could save the birds.

The birds were all depressed. Loro was now aware he earned the ire of all the other birds in all the other cages. The other nine parrots threw accusing glances at him for he could have helped the boy win the race if he had coached the boy at once.

Deervana, hopeless of saving the forest, stared at the boy with so much anger. Nevertheless, as the moderator, she had to name Tenten as the winner. It was time for her to announce the winner's prize when Rebmun stood up to intervene.

"Hold it!," Rebmun raised his hand and stood up to Deervana's surprise. She wondered what was the boy going to protest.

All the birds waited anxiously. They held their breaths in their eagerness to hear what the boy would be saying next while Loro wondered: *What is he up to?*

"Honorable moderator, you cannot award the prize to my opponent. Not even a single bird would be awarded to him."

"Did you hear that?" Loro asked his companions with excitement. "The boy said the winner of the race can't have his prize. We all be freed from the giant's custody!"

"I repeat for clarification, the winner of this race can't have his prize!" Rebmun repeated his conclusion. "I'm basing my conclusion on what the giant laid out."

"The boy is really silly . . ." one parrot said.

"Noooo! The little boy is genuinely smart!" another parrot responded.

All the birds in the cages inside the cave fell silent. They were all confused of Rebmun's point yet nobody raised a voice. In the midst of their silence, the giant shouted his protest.

"That doesn't make sense, Nerdo! That doesn't make sense!"

"Let me remind the moderator that the last number the winner said was 'zero' and . . ." Rebmun paused, waiting for the birds' cheer; none did. "And the rule says that the winner can only have the number of birds that corresponds to the last number the winner mentioned. The winner said "zero" which means nothing."

This time, the birds applauded.

"It was because the procedure was changed," the giant vehemently reasoned out. "He was counting up and I was doing the reverse to give this stupid boy an edge over me! The procedure was changed!"

"Yeah, the procedure was changed but the rule stayed the same," the moderator refuted.

There was silence again until one of the birds raised his voice: Then what's the verdict?

"The boy is right. In fairness to both contestants, it should be known to everybody that on this day, in the race of counting numbers in the forest of Deervana, although Tenten won the game, he couldn't have the prize at stake. As logic dictates, zero means nothing so not a single bird could be awarded to the winner."

All the birds inside the cave cheered again. "That's amazing," the parrots chorused.

"Therefore," the doe concluded, "all the birds in the cave should have to be released free from Tenten's custody."

Everybody was silent in their eagerness to hear more words of goodwill from the doe.

"However, let this be put on records in the history of my domain that Tenten won the game, but only the honor should be awarded to him not the prize at stake according to the rule that was laid out by the winner himself. All the birds then must be set free."

Tenten believed the boy pulled a trick in changing the procedure of the contest. Or something was wrong when he laid the rules but pride prevented him to say more complaints. It was his fault after all for consenting without fully analyzing the procedure that the boy laid out. It came blurry to Tenten, but the giant pretended to have understood everything to impress everybody that he was really smart as the boy had said.

XIX

The giant was so proud of himself but didn't know where his failure was. Now he was duped, out-smarted by the little imp whom he called a "silly brat" and a "dumb head".

Uncivilized as he was, Tenten knew how to honor agreements. With his strength he could have gone against the rule but it was he who made it and he agreed to the procedure that Rebmun laid down. Embarrassed, the giant walked down empty-handed for not even a single bird was awarded to him.

The giant disappeared behind the woods leaving everybody in the forest of Deervana celebrating.

The birds cheered on the sight of Rebmun approaching the cave to release them in abidance to the contest rule.

"This calls for a celebration," the doe joyfully announced. "There's a lot of food to feast on the trees."

Once released from their cages, the birds flew happily all over the place hopping from tree to tree while they pecked insects and worms crawling in the twigs and branches of the trees.

"This forest will come to life again," Rebmun told Deervana. "In a few days, sprouts will spring again in all the trees around."

"Thank you for your help, little boy. If you think of visiting us in the future, you're always welcome here."

"I may be back but don't know when. I'd like to see your constituents returning home."

"Definitely they would come back. The wind will tell them that everything is doing well again in this forest they call home. You may stay for another day if you want to meet them. They will be happy and excited to see a hero."

"I have to come to my own home now. If I can't bring Loro back on the seventh day after he left, I can't have my long planned vacation. Today is the seventh day."

"So Loro can't stay any longer."

"I wish he could," said Rebmun. "Anyway, Loro has his own home."

"Is it in a cage? Are you putting him in a cage like Tenten did?"

"He's safe there and doesn't have to look for his own food. Loro will be okay."

"Poor Loro will be in prison again and he has to eat whatever food you give for he has no choice. I was hoping you'd let him stay with us here in the forest. What future awaits him in a cage? Is life worth living without freedom?"

Deervana's questions plunged Rebmun into deep thoughts. The doe was right for now he saw how happy Loro was playing with the other birds. Like him, he realized how beautiful it was to be absolutely free when he slipped out of home to look for the lorikeet. But with the bird back to his cage at home, Rebmun could have a happy summer vacation that he always wanted to have even if at Loro's expense. But what if the parrot doesn't want to return?

Rebmun whistled for Loro. Immediately, the bird swooped down and perched at the boy's right wrist.

"It's getting late and I'm going home now. Do you want to come home with me?" Rebmun asked the bird.

"Do I have a choice?" Loro asked in return.

"You have the choice but if I can't get you back home tonight, I couldn't have that trip to Disney World that I always have wanted. That's the condition my parents imposed but I'll give you freedom to choose."

Rebmun saw the joy in the face of the lorikeet, but it seemed the bird couldn't say what he really wanted.

"Here's a deal," Rebmun continued. "If you come home with me, I will talk to my parents to grant you freedom. They won't turn me down."

"Great! Home for me is not necessarily this forest. It could be on the tree near your room. I still can wake you up at six in the morning."

"Naaahhh. I won't need your counting anymore," Rebmun said raising his left arm.

Loro's eyes beamed with wonder seeing what Rebmun was wearing.

"Wow! That's a watch! You have a wristwatch! Can you read the time?"

"Of course! I'm getting serious with numbers, my

friend. I have realized how important numbers are in everyone's life."

"Cool! How come you lost the race?"

"I got nervous. Why didn't you help me right away when I was in trouble?"

"Same thing; I also got tense," Loro said.

"All's well that ends well," Deervana, who was listening to the duo's conversation, remarked. "Tenten won the race but the birds are freed. Rebmun outsmarted the giant with a simple trick."

"The giant deserved it for misjudging me," the boy replied.

"Overconfidence on himself made him misjudge you," said Deervana. "That gives us a lesson: Never underestimate your opponents."

XX

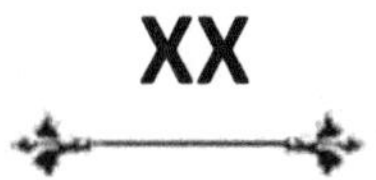

The late afternoon sun was about to touch the western hemisphere. Once more, the doe thanked Rebmun and Miles for helping her save the forest.

Rebmun took the first step towards home. Miles followed him with Loro flying low beside the dog.

"Be safe on your way out. Watch each other's back. It's almost dark. The way towards the exit of this forest could be dangerous to the newcomers," Deervana shouted at the group.

The boy, the bird, and the dog went on walking. They hardly reached halfway to the exit of the forest when Rebmun thought of resting on a stump along the trail. The boy was recollecting how he was able to bring up the idea that technically defeated the giant in the race and enabled him to save the birds.

The remaining rays of the afternoon sun were almost gone when Rebmun thought of continuing the journey. He was about to stand when all of a sudden he saw a big black hawk coming out of nowhere rushing towards their direction. The boy sensed danger. He instantly remembered the hawk in his dream that grabbed Loro in his sleep and brought him back to the *Field of Pines.*

Impulsively, the boy shouted at Loro to dodge but the hawk had grasped Loro's head in its claws. The hawk was ascending but Loro was able to transform himself into Poutric. The sudden change in his weight pulled the hawk down; it was descending to the ground. Seeing his chance, Miles crouched and leaped at the hawk catching its neck between his teeth.

As soon as Miles touched the ground, he swished the hawk with all his might and struck it hard against the trunk of a huge oak tree. The hawk was slammed to the ground as Dargo; his neck bleeding profusely.

Taking advantage of the situation, Miles jumped at Dargo once again. The dark warrior got hold of Miles's neck. He tried to strangle the dog. Both rolled down the hill before the eyes of Rebmun who seemed shocked with that sudden event.

Dargo grabbed a big stone and struck the dog's head; he missed. When he was about to hit Miles again, a blue eagle swept down and instantly shot Dargo with a plume-like dagger hitting his right arm. It forced Dargo to release Miles from his hold. The blue eagle descended to the ground and it surprised Poutric when he saw it wasn't Yorka but Rafos.

"Rafos," Poutric called. "How did you turn yourself into an eagle?"

Rafos got no time to answer. The bloodied Dargo had pulled off the dagger from his right arm and stabbed Rafos at his back like what he did to Yorka.

Rebmun and Poutric were watching the former buddies squared up to a long fist fight, competing against each other in strength and in skill that was aborted in Rebmun's dream. Both were wounded but each one had his own advantageous moments, one after the other.

In the long run, Rafos was able to overpower the strength of his opponent. Rebmun got a rope from his backpack and with Poutric's help tied Dargo to a tree.

At this point, a giant vulture swept in followed by the thirteen guzzlers carrying Mimosa; her hands tied at her back. The giant vulture transformed itself into Varcoba.

"Stop there," Rafos warned her. "Release Mimosa right now or I'll be forced to kill your most trusted guard!"

"You may do so if you wish," Varcoba replied. "His life isn't much of importance in this situation. All I want is the amulet."

"Is this what I get in return of my services and loyalty?" Dargo yelled at Varcoba as he was angered of what Varcoba said.

"You're a lame duck, Dargo. What for do I need your services?" Varcoba replied with a mock at her erstwhile friend. "I don't want useless friends."

"Damn you! I worked so hard for you!"

"Say whatever you want; I'd been doomed to hell from the very beginning. Next time, Dargo, be careful on whom to trust."

"Next time I meet you, Varcoba, I swear that would be your end."

"That's if you come out of here alive. But it seems you won't," Varcoba laughed again. "Look at you. How pathetic you had become."

"We'll see each other again and by that time get yourself ready for my revenge. You and your disciples and your guzzlers will suffer my wrath."

In reply, Varcoba freed again a sardonic laughter. "Do as you wish," Varcoba dared ignoring Dargo's threat.

"You're wasting my time, Varcoba," Rafos butted in. "I want you to release Mimosa right now before darkness closes in."

"Hey, Rafos, I will release Mimosa in exchange of Yorka's talisman. Hand it to me right now before I release your princess!"

"I don't have it!"

"Why don't you ask Poutric? Your wonder boy is keeping it."

"Give her the amulet, Poutric," Rafos commanded without looking at the teenage lad. "Save your sister and let's get out of here."

"I don't have it," answered Poutric.

"There you go again, liar. I saw you having it before you turned into a parrot and fled."

"I lost it on my way out of the Kingdom of Dome," Poutric shouted.

"This is not a good time to lie," shouted the evil lady; her crumpled face was fuming with anger. "Which matters more – your sister's life or the amulet of Yorka?"

"Don't listen to her Poutric," Mimosa interrupted.

"You know what kind of evil she is. She doesn't know how to honor her words."

"There's venom in your tongue, young lady. I can have it cut to pieces if I wish to," Varcoba warned.

"You should have done that long time ago when I didn't have the strength and courage to fight you back. The day you attacked the Kingdom of Dome and killed my parents is still fresh in my mind."

"If you've known me since that day, then you know well how vicious I could be."

"You can't scare me! I have trained myself how to match your strength and power! Now I'm ready for this encounter. I will bring your end and I will not let this chance pass by!"

"That is if I grant you that chance! Poor Mimosa, you're wasting your life waiting for the chance that will never be yours for I will not let this day pass by without seeing you gasping for your last breath."

"Do as you wish, Varcoba, but you never find the amulet," Poutric interfered.

"You're keeping it in your gullet, Poutric. Don't let me slash your throat."

"Do it, but you have to catch me first."

Immediately, Poutric changed himself again to a bird and flew away. Varcoba turned herself back to a vulture and gave the lorikeet a chase.

It was when Deervana came to the scene followed by the hundred birds that Rebmun rescued from Tenten. The flock swarmed towards Varcoba's guards and thirteen guzzlers who were guarding the captive Mimosa. The birds gave Rafos and Miles the courage to fight with them. Varcoba's guards and guzzlers were no match against the fierceness of the birds. In the long run, the guards gave up and ran away. The thirteen guzzlers, seeing the guards giving up the fight, also had gone to nowhere.

Rafos untied Mimosa while Varcoba was chasing Poutric in and out the forest.

Up over the top of the trees Poutric and Varcoba vanished from Rebmun's sight but not long after, they were back inside the woods with the vulture still chasing the lorikeet. Loro playfully flew around the trees, laughing on seeing he had left the vulture quite a good distance. The giant black bird was running out of vigor. She was breathing hard so she rested on a branch as she turned herself as Varcoba. Loro perched on a branch of another tree not too far that he could watch Varcoba's movement. He turned himself into the lad that Poutric was.

"What's wrong, Varcoba?" Poutric shouted as he watched the evil woman catching her breathe. "Ahhh . . . you're out of breath. Let me guess . . .

you're having chest pains and headaches and dizziness! That's stress. You're sick. Yeah, you need to give yourself a rest."

"I have never been sick, moron. I'm stronger than your strongest zobus!"

"You, queen of denials, you only have the guts but don't have the vigor."

"So what?"

"It hurts, Varcoba, to know that you are an overstaying tenant in this planet. It's time for you to exit from this world. Give yourself a complete rest in hell."

"It's not funny, idiot, it's not funny!" Varcoba screamed; her face distorting.

"Calm down. You're in danger if you forgot to take your medicine for high blood." Poutric said and laughed sardonically.

Rebmun grinned at Poutric's words. He remembered telling Loro about his dad feeling so bad when he forgot to take his medicine.

Varcoba stared at Poutric with her red bulging eyes. The disrespectful boy was only making fun of her and was enjoying it.

I've got to chew up this bastard, Varcoba thought. She gazed at Poutric with so much intensities. *I must chew him up.*

Gaining back resilience, Varcoba turned into a vulture again. As Poutric was always prepared to counteract what Varcoba could do next, he turned himself into a parrot in a flash and fled before the vulture could.

For some moments, the tiny lorikeet and the huge vulture were chasing around the trees. This time, the vulture wasn't as energized as earlier but never had lost the tiny bird from her sight. The vulture was flying closer behind.

"I'm coming! This time you can never outfly me! You can never hide yourself from me! Poor Poutric, on this day you'll be declared dead."

The vulture tried to snatch the parrot's tail; she missed. The parrot laughed harder as he flew around that made Varcoba angrier.

She admitted to herself that she no longer have the vigor that could match the energy of the boy. She must give herself a rest. The big black vulture hurriedly perched on the huge stone beneath an old oak tree and turned herself back as Varcoba.

XXI

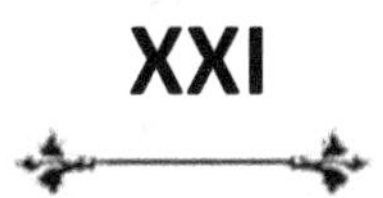

Finding out that the vulture had stopped chasing him, the parrot perched as Poutric on the branch of the old oak tree directly above where Varcoba was resting.

All the while, Poutric kept pestering about Varcoba's inability to outsmart him.

Varcoba was keeping an eye at the boy while keeping her silence. Her evil mind was working on how to find a good chance to catch the mischievous Poutric.

Believing that the lad was fully unaware of her moves, Varcoba turned herself back to a huge vulture, and in a quick ascent snatched the boy's leg. It was late for Poutric to transform himself into a bird.

Immediately, the vulture flew upward tugging Poutric in his claws with the thought of dropping the boy in the most unsafe place she could find.

As Rafos and Mimosa were closely watching them, not wasting a second, Rafos handed his sword to Mimosa and turned himself into a blue eagle. Quickly enough, Mimosa jumped unto the eagle's back. The eagle gave the vulture a chase.

"You don't have to come with me, Mimosa. This isn't safe for you."

"Grant me this chance, Rafos. It's been a long time I've wished to exact my vengeance on Varcoba for the death of my parents. She must have to pay for all the bad things she did to the Kingdom of Dome."

"That evil woman is immortal. The best we can do is gang her up and bring her to Rebmun. The boy knows what punishment does Varcoba deserve."

"Deervana's birds can help us tie Varcoba. They have the ropes of Tenten."

Flapping his wings faster following the vulture's trail, the blue eagle got closer above the giant black bird. Seeing her chance, Mimosa quickly jumped to the back of the vulture. That made her lost its balance and loosened her hold on Poutric.

The boy was released from the claw of the vulture and was falling down but as fast as he went, the blue eagle swiftly descended and caught Poutric's hand. The boy climbed to the blue eagle's neck from where he watched how his sister wrestled the vulture.

Mimosa raised her sword up high with a long leap and thrusted down the sword at the vulture's nape. The vulture lost its balance once again. Mimosa fell off from the vulture's back but was able to catch it's leg and there she hang on while the vulture was swirling fast down to the ground.

With Mimosa still clinging on the vulture's leg, it fell into a hill of dried leaves. Instantly, the vulture transformed itself back as Varcoba just in time that the blue eagle landed nearby and turned itself back to Rafos. Being both unarmed, the two fierce foes were using bare hands. Rafos got more advantage; he had been excellent in wrestling as he learned it from Yorka.

Poutric was confident Rafos could overcome Varcoba's power. At first, Varcoba was no match to the tricks that Rafos used. Yet, using her evil power, she was in the verge of outfighting the most stalwart in the Kingdom of Dome.

Rafos was losing his strength. Finding him too weak to fight the evil Varcoba, Deervana commanded the birds to swarm around the evil lady who was no match against the strength of Deervana's birds. They tied her whole body using the ropes of Tenten.

Varcoba lost her evil power. Deervana's birds tied Varcoba to the biggest oak tree nearer to Rebmun while waiting for his judgment.

"Hopefully, now that Varcoba's power is gone, I hope the Field of Pines will attain peace and progress throughout the years," Rafos told Mimosa after he summoned all the surviving zobuses to gather around.

"As you all know, the power of Varcoba is over," Mimosa announced. Her voice was almost buried in the deafening cheers of the zobuses. "Tomorrow, we all come to the Dome to celebrate our victory. May our tribe grow from this day on and the curse to extinct our race may completely vanish."

Another cheers exploded.

"I'm designating my brother Poutric to take care of Yorka's amulet. That makes him the official keeper of the kingdom's safety."

As you wish, my dear sister, I'll be following your order but let's not forget to acknowledge the help of Rafos. Without him, we couldn't have regained the Kingdom of Dome." Poutric said.

"But of course. It's high time that we have to ac-knowledge Rafos as the foremost hero of the Field of Pines. He had been there for us on those times the other kingdoms of the dark world were attack-ing us."

"By the way, Rafos how did you turn yourself into a blue eagle?" Poutric asked.

"I learned it from Yorka. He said that I can turn myself into a blue eagle as he did even without the amulet. All I need is to say the magic word."

"What's the magic word?" Rebmun asked even if he already knew.

"I'm not supposed to tell that to anybody, not even to Poutric or Mimosa. Yorka made me promise to keep it confidential no matter what happens."

"I think I know it! I know the magic word," Reb-mun shouted out. Poutric feared the boy would say the word. He should have not told the boy about it.

"What is it?" Rafos asked half-believing.

"Don't mind him, Rafos," Poutric interfered. "The boy thinks the magic word is 'abracadabra'." Poutric forced himself to laugh. "The boy knows nothing from the *Field of Pines*."

"Okay . . . enough with this discussion," said Mi-mosa. "The day had ended. We must go back to the Kingdom of Dome for the celebration of the victory we achieved today."

"But before anything else," Poutric interfered. "We'll hear what my buddy Rebmun wants to do with this traitor and this creature from hell," Poutric said and ordered the birds to bring Varcoba in front of Rebmun for sentencing. "The whole Kingdom of Dome would always acknowledge Rebmun's help. We owe our Fate largely to him."

Rafos pushed Dargo nearer to Varcoba who was standing in front of Rebmun, waiting for the boy's judgment. Varcoba wasn't a bit worried of what's to happen next while the wounded Dargo was groaning not only for his pain, but his anger at Varcoba.

"Stop whining, Dargo. You are a seasoned warrior and you're supposed to be immune of pain," Varcoba told her erstwhile trusted man. "Spend your last minutes praying for the interference of the lord from hell that the boy sentences you to a sudden execution. Only in death that you'll be relieved from pain."

"I will see to it that you'll suffer the same fate," Dargo moaned. "You'll die first . . ."

"You forgot that nobody can ever kill me! Nobody, not even the lord from hell!"

"Let's see! Once the boy banishes you to oblivion, you'll never be heard of again. You'll be history in the Field of Pines."

While the two captives were at each other's rage, Rebmun was thinking on what to do with them. Wearily, he rested back on a big stump along the trail thinking on what punishment he should impose for the assault the two invaders had done.

"Come on, Master. It's almost six O'clock," Loro said. The bird wondered what Rebmun was stopping for when total darkness was about to cover the forest. "It's getting dark. Per Deervana, it's not safe for us to walk in the woods at night."

"Hey, we cannot just leave these prisoners here. We can neither bring them home nor leave them to Deervana. And we cannot execute them or free them just like that. You better help me think on what to do with them?"

"Who are you talking about?" Loro asked in surprise as he looked around.

Rebmun stood up and did the same. No one else was there other than the dog and the parrot. "Where are they?" he asked.

"What they? If you mean the birds, they're already freed and Tenten had gone back to nowhere. Everything's over. Hey, are you alright, buddy boy?"

"They were here . . . Varcoba and Dargo and Rafos and Mimosa . . . they were here just seconds ago," Rebmun said and looked around once more. "And you, Loro . . . you were a teenage lad with the name of Poutric, isn't it?"

"As I told you before, in the world I came from I bear the name of Poutric. The persons you mentioned aren't here with us. They're in the Field of Pines. You never had seen them for they never had been here yet. You were only building images, but how did you know their names?"

They were in my dream, Rebmun thought.

It was then Rebmun realized that the events he had witnessed minutes earlier which seemed so real were but products of his imagination based on the dream he had had. He concluded that was all hallucinations. He remembered Loro telling him that Varcoba and her group were in the village of Moon Cap in search of him. That was Loro's hallucinations. Now he realized that there never was a Dargo, no Rafos, no Varcoba, and no Mimosa. He didn't see Deervana and saw no birds around but only the lorikeet. *What's happening?* Rebmun asked himself.

The boy felt embarrassed as he was getting himself involved with those images that Loro planted in his mind. He wasn't any different from Loro who was fond of imagining weird characters and impossible sceneries. Based on those characters, he made a fantastic story that was unbelievable to happen in his time. Yet, it seemed so real. He wondered: Was Loro telling him the truth? Does the Field of Pines really exist? The boy thought he needs to find it out.

"Well, let's move on; it's getting dark," Rebmun told his pets.

From his backpack, Rebmun fished out a mini flashlight and looked at his wrist watch. *Time to go home,* he thought; it was six O'clock and inside the forest of Deervana, the trail back home was already dark.

-END-

www.ingramcontent.com/pod-product-compliance
Lightning Source LLC
Chambersburg PA
CBHW070732030726
47601CB00001B/2